The Best Laid Plans ...

& Other stories

Sue Lord

Published by Sue LordPrinted by Createspace – an Amazon Company

For My Family

With thanks to Susan Falkingham

And

My Webb Footed Friend

1 The best laid plans...

2 Payment

3 Nicked

4 Taking the piss

5 Country pursuits

6 Friends

7 Uncle Bill

8 Skipper

9 Fair's fair

10 The evils of drink

11 Public transport

12 Amateurs

13 Perverts

14 The Cafe

15 Coal Tar Soap

16 Religion

17 Sailing

18 Murder?

19 Good ideas, not

20 Weddings

21 Retirement

1

THE BEST LAID PLANS…

Listen. Let's get this straight. I'm a robber, not a thief. I never burgle people's homes, shoplift or mug any one, that's all you need to know about me really.

Now, my mate Mal, he can fix any motor and he's magic with a welding torch. He's got a yard on the edge of a wood, up a dirt track, and the right tools for the job, cutting equipment and that. So, when Ginger got this tip, about a safe going begging on a Wednesday. Mal sprang to mind.

'Sweet innit? Good amount of money me-thinks' I said to Ginger and he said "Yeah."

Well, he would have agreed with anything.

Pissed as a proverbial.

We had a toast ... 'to a good plan.' I said.

'And all who sail in her,' Ginger slurred.

*

Next day I jumped in the Range Rover and beetled off up to Mal's yard to run my idea past him. It hadn't rained for weeks so the motor got dusty instead of covered in the usual mud going up the track. You have to be grateful for small mercies don't you?

Mal wasn't about, nor was Tracy, his wife. So, I lit up, sat on a straw bale and took in nature, by way of a few moth eaten old nags standing about in one of the fields. And I could tell that the sheep, shut in a stable behind me, weren't all that happy. I stuck my head over the door and told them to shut up. They looked at me all hurt like. You could become a veggie at times like that, if you were so inclined.

There's a lot of shit about in this nature game. Too much for my liking I can tell you, and quite a bit of it sticks to your shoes. I decided not to hang around since the tractor wasn't there.

I figured Mal was out pursuing his hobby, namely driving a tractor round the lanes and through the woods. He likes to peer into parked cars at courting couples. I think he invented dogging. Now, Mal is an ugly man and not a bit of his body hasn't got a tattoo on it. Give you a nasty turn it would, seeing his face leering in at you just as you were about to get stuck in.

I stood on my fag end and turned to go. As I walked back to the wheels I heard a tractor come up the track, spluttering away, with black smoke pouring out the chimney style exhaust pipe. As it got nearer, I could see that Tracy was giving Mal the ear-ole. Her head was wagging fit to fall off. She jumped down from the cab and looked me over like I'd just crawled out from under a stone or something.

'Oh. It's you.' She said.

'It is.' I said. 'You're looking ravishing today Tracy, if I may be so bold.'

She squinted at me with her little, piggy blue eyes, which are so close together they almost meet in the middle. I gazed, as usual, at the two hairs that sprouted out of a mole on her chin. It always fascinated me that. One is straight and the other's curly.

'Bugger off.' Tracy said, as she walked past me into the stable yard. The smell of her particular brand of perfume wafted up my nose as she passed. 'Old Manure,' by the

'House of Horse,' dabbed behind the ears.

I wondered what colour the stripes of her puffer jacket had once been and then imagined getting into bed with her. I shivered and crossed myself as she disappeared into a stable. Mal and I didn't speak, just watched the space where she'd been. I expect we were thinking much the same thing.

I opened my mouth to speak but she hove back into sight.

'Don't you go skulking off wiv 'im. Mal. You gotta fetch fucking Sharmain

from school at half past free!' Tracy shouted, as she dragged some poor bugger of a horse out towards the fields.

'She needs a smacking mate.' I said.

'Take a braver man than me.' Mal grinned, showing his green teeth. He scratched himself through his grey string vest. His eyes filled up half his face. Mal's milk bottle bottom glasses make him look like a Bush Baby. He smells more of motor oil, with just a touch of the eau de manure.

'What can I do for you then?' He put his hand in his trouser pocket and scratched his balls.

'Well. Ginger's got some info and I've come up with a plan. We need a man of your talents. Should be a lot of money coming to us on Wednesday.'

I outlined my idea.

'Yeah!' He took off his specs and polished them on his vest. His eyes went back to normal size. 'Who's getting the car?'

'Snatch.'

'No! You're barking!' Mal put the bins back on and his eyes took up half his face again. He scratched the greasy bald patch at the top of his head. 'You know he ain't with it at the moment what with the twins teething an' all. He isn't getting his sleep. A bloke needs his kip.'

'Yeah. Well. He's down on his luck and Mandy's up the stick again.' I shrugged, 'He's got muscle, and we'll need it.'

'You're too soft, that's your trouble.' Mal picked his nose without much success I should think, since he bites his nails down to the quick.

'Snatch could do with a bit of something in his head to go with his biceps.' Mal said as he inspected the top of his finger. 'Must keep his brains in his pants. You'd think Mandy would cut it off.' Mal gave a leery laugh and wiped his hand on his trousers. 'We've got some gelding stuff. Think they'd like to lend it?'

'Not till we've pulled this one off. No.'

'MAL! Watchya doin!' Tracy's delicate tones rang out across three fields. 'Time you went to fetch fucking Sharmain?'

'I'd better go mate. Me life won't be worth living.' Mal climbed into his old Land Rover. 'Snatch better get the car by Monday if you want to do the job on Wednesday night, case there's a problem. See ya.' Mal left in a cloud of black smoke and dust, a one-man pollution machine.

I lit a fag as Tracy came up behind me.

'What you two cookin up then?'

'Just passing the time of day Tracy.' I said, trying to be friendly. 'What's in the buckets?'

'Shit. What do you think it is? Caviar?' She gave me the old Margaret

Thatcher look. 'I've got to get on. Some of us has to work for a living.'

'I suppose a quick shag is out of the

question then?'

I didn't mean it. It just sort of slipped out.

'Fuck off.'

You have to smile don't you? Tracy clanked off across the yard and I climbed into the Range Rover. I contemplated her bum as I started up the motor. He's a brave man, is Mal one way and another.

*

It was Monday, late evening. Ginger and I were sitting in 'The Feathers' when the phone behind the bar rang. The landlord called me over. It was Snatch. He'd got the wheels sorted and Mal had started work.

'It's sweet, Ginger. All sorted. This calls for a vodka.'

I watched him toddle off to the bar.

He's as bald as a coot is Ginger. Like a boiled egg his head is. In fact he hasn't got a hair on his body.

Total alopecia.

He's called Ginger because when he went into the army for his national service, he grew a mop of curly ginger hair, amazing innit? Could have had a beard, but it wasn't allowed. Course when he left, all the hair fell out, but the name stuck.

Ginger is a big man with hands like bunches of bananas and a broken nose, not a man to argue with.

He breeds budgies! Tiny little things, the chicks, funny to see them great paws of his lifting up tiny little baby birds. They're not scared of him not a bit... He scares me sometimes.

Me and Ginger went up the yard next morning. No sign of Tracy. Mal came out of one of the sheds rubbing his hands with a rag.

'Watcha! I've finished it. You can give me a hand with the mattress.'

'Where's Tracy?' I asked.

'Gone buying some horses. She went early. Don't worry. She hasn't seen anything.'

Ginger looked round the fields. 'I don't like bloody horses. You can't trust them.' He polished his head. 'Should be in tins of cat food, best place for them.'

Good job Tracy wasn't there.

We followed Mal into the barn. The car was

parked in the middle, all covered up. Mal made like a magician as he pulled off the tarpaulins. 'Dah dah!'

'Stone me!' said Ginger. 'Bloody 'ell,' says I. 'Snatch got it from down the

college.' Mall rubbed his hand along the window ledge. 'Some poor bugger worked hard on this.'

And they had too. It was an ancient Beetle. Bright yellow, not exactly inconspicuous, not with the scarlet, orange and lime green flowers. Not to mention the purple 'Ban the bomb' signs on the sides.

I wondered what the thinking was behind the choice of motor? Could it be Snatch thought, "Double bluff?" Plod would never credit any right-minded villain pulling a job in a car like that? Or perhaps, Snatch thought hand knitted, hippie types are not suspicious, since they spend their lives in a drug induced haze of peace, love and lentils.'

But let's face it; if Snatch had a brain, he'd be dangerous.

Mal had cut the top off; made a good job of it too.

'Is it going to be big enough?' I wondered.

'Yeah. Fit like a glove.'

Ginger took out the back seat. We pushed the front seats forward as far as they would go. Mal dragged a mattress out of the back of his Land rover.

'Bloody 'ell it stinks.' Ginger said as we manhandled it into the car.

Ginger was not wrong. It had come from a skip outside some old peoples' home. Mal said he hadn't noticed a smell. I wouldn't be surprised to find Mal had no sense of smell at all.

I gave Mal a fag and we leaned back and viewed our work.

'Sweet,' he said. 'Where's Ginger gone?'

Ginger had gone for a slash.

When he came back he had a tiny kitten in his hand.

'Can I have it, Mal?'

'Yeah. If you want it mate. It belongs to the stray cat that lives in the back of the old horsebox. But won't it tuck in to your birds when it grows up?'

'I'll teach it not to, won't I?'

Right, some hope, I thought. Mal looked at Ginger as if he had grown another head.

So, on the way home we had to stop off and buy cat litter, little toy mice, bowls and stuff. The daft bugger even bought it a purple bed and matching scratching post.

'What are you going call it then.' I asked. 'Marmalade?'

'Nah! ... Ginger of course.'

Of course, silly me!

*

Wednesday night didn't start too well.

Snatch was driving the Bug, me in the front. Ginger had to sit on the mattress in the back. He was moaning about the smell. Ginger Jnr was wailing in a cardboard box, he didn't want to leave the kitten at home, seems it was a bit off colour.

So, there we were, three girt great men wearing black balaclavas, sitting in a psychedelic mini with the top cut out, our knees up to our ears. It was raining so Ginger put up the red and white golfing umbrella that he had 'found' in the pub.Off we went. That's when we realised that the Beetle was a bit underpowered, it needed a de-coke. Needed a bloody new engine to be precise.

'Bit of a dog innit?' I said. 'We must have done the owner a favour nicking this. Collect the insurance won't he?'

Snatch doubted it, since the car wasn't taxed. Odds on it wasn't insured either. 'Great' I said and stuck my head in my hands.

Ginger told Snatch to step on it but not break the speed limit. 'Some bloody hope.' I sighed. Eventually we arrived at the betting shop.Snatch shunted backwards and forwards to get the car into the right position, Ginger and I shouting over the noise of the engine.

"To me! To him!"

We got it about right and Snatch switched off. The silence, as they say in books, was deafening. All except for the kitten, which was trying to tear its way out of the box and screaming its head off. Ginger left it in the back of the car.

You don't need to know how we got in, tricks of the trade. We took the stairs to the second floor. The office door was locked.

No problem.

Snatch and I went in and had a look round.

'Where's Ginger?' he whispered.

We shone the torches about, perplexed.
Then we heard the sound of running water.

We breathed in and stood still.

The sound of footsteps came towards the
office door...

Ginger came in with a plastic jug and began
to water the plants in the reception area. He
looked at us, goggling at him, speechless.

'It's criminal' he said 'what people do to
living things.'

We found the safe, a big black old-
fashioned job.

'Must be full of money,' Ginger rubbed his
hands together. 'Big race today.'

The three of us eventually got it over to the
window. With a bit more sweat and heaving
we got it up onto the window ledge. We
lined it up with the car below and dropped
it.

A direct hit you could say.

'The bloody kitten!' I said. 'Whoops!' Said
Snatch.

'Jnr!' Croaked Ginger.

He began to run, knocking chairs and stuff out of his way.

We charged down the stairs after him.

As Snatch and I rounded the door we ran straight into Ginger who had stopped dead. We peered round him. The safe had dropped neatly into the car all right, but the wheels had splayed out.

A little bit of the cardboard box stuck out from under the safe.

Tears soaked into Ginger's balaclava.

'Whoops.' Snatch said.

Ginger grabbed his collar and drew back his fist. 'If you say that again I'll ... Junior!'

We all heard the familiar wail. The kitten jumped up onto the dashboard, looked at us with disgust and began to wash its face. No cardboard box would hold that kitten. In the distance we heard the familiar sound of a police car.

'Let's go to Scab's place,' I said.

We could get a cuppa up at his scrap yard and he was lined up to crush the car for us.

We walked briskly away from the scene. Scabs office was in a comfy mobile home at the back of his scrap yard. He kips there when his old lady throws him out. He also uses it as a poker school and it's a good place to take a bit of skirt on a Friday night. The key was kept under an old oil drum by the door.

We had to play hunt the kitten because it jumped out of the window. When we finally found it, Ginger shoved it into a sack and said he had decided to call it Lucky. It was lucky. Lucky that the guard dogs were chained up!

So anyway, we had a fry up, followed by a game of cribbage. At about seven we fried some more bacon and Scabs came in rubbing his hands.

'Well lads, what did you get then?'

'We won't be keeping you in spot cream that's for sure.' I said.

'Pour yourself a cuppa.' Ginger pointed to the teapot. 'Have a bacon sarney and we'll tell you all about it.'

*

The next evening D. I. Baines, came into 'The Feathers'. He walked over to our table, grinning like the proverbial.

'Guess what?'"What?'We found a Beetle outside a betting shop. It had a safe in it.'

'Really?' I said, 'That is strange, Mr Baines.''Don't expect you know anything about it?'

'Nah,' Ginger shook his head and took a pull at his beer.'

I gave Baines a baffled look.

'Someone went to a lot of trouble.' Baines looked solemn. Then he began to chuckle. 'The owner tells me the safe only had a hundred quid and some old Playboys inside."

You have to laugh, don't you?

2

PAYMENT

Now, I might be a robber but I don't rip off my friends and I consider a deal's a deal. So when a couple of pikey brothers asked me to clear a site. I said 'Okeydokey,' gave them a price, and we shook on it.

Now, these brothers had run a garden centre for a good few years, a run–down place, but in a good position. Well, they had come into some money. I believe they looked after some bullion for a bloke. Say no more.Anyway, they could hardly put the money in the bank, could they? The brothers decided to expand and build a posh new garden centre.

There was a derelict farmhouse and stables

on the site, three big glasshouses, old sheds and loads of rubbish. The original buildings were listed, so I got Snatch to back the J.C.B. into them, by mistake, of course. Same with a couple of trees that were growing where the coffee shop was going.

I did "the muck away," Snatch and Ginger did what they do best, knock things down.

In the centre of the site was a girt great concrete pond, full of Coi Carp. It was one of the brother's pride and joy.

"Them fish are worth thousands of pounds a piece," he told me, all proud. We had to be careful not to upset them, vibrations and all that. The fish and the fancy birds that the other brother collected were going to be the main attractions. Ginger talked to the birds and covered the pond every morning to stop the dust going in.

We finished the job on time and I went to collect our money. One brother lived in a bungalow at the back of the site. The other lived over the road. The bungalows were exactly the same.

Lion's heads on the gateposts, electric gates, herringbone drive. High walls, with hanging baskets all filled with red and yellow flowers. They had quadruple, electric 'up and over' garage doors and a swimming pool with sauna in the back garden.

The doorbell played 'Love me Tender.'
Smart.

A ropey looking blond opened the door. She had the biggest chest I've seen in years, all bobbling about, like it had a life of its own. I am not sure if it was all her own work, if you know what I mean.

Done up to the nines she was, in something short and shiny with shoulder pads. Her high heels had the same colour bows. She had a huge hat in her hands that she put on and did a twirl.

'What da yer think?'

'Great...' I said. 'Very pink.'

'We're all going to Ascot tomorrow. Ladies day ain't it?'

'Sweet.' I said 'I've come for my money.'She showed me into the lounge.

One end of the room was taken up by the bar, optics on the wall with pink silk flowers wound into the wrought iron work. The room was very pink too. The guy came out of the billiard room next door with a plastic carrier bag in his hand. He emptied it onto a glass table and I began to count the money.

He had gold sovereigns on every finger, a couple hanging round his neck and one hanging off his gold Rolex. He had his name engraved onto a heavy gold bracelet. And just so he couldn't forget it, his name was also tattooed onto the fingers of his left hand. On his right hand was the name Lucy.

'It isn't all here.' I pointed out. 'It's a fifteen hundred short.'

'Yeah, well I ain't been to the bank, 'ave I? Go over and get the rest from me brother.'

Now his brother has a reputation of being something of a nutter but money is a money innit?

*

I returned with Ginger and Snatch as a precaution and pressed the buzzer on the gatepost.

'Yeah!' The pikey nutter didn't sound too happy.

I explained that we had come for the rest of our money. It was difficult to hear him over the barking and snarling of the two Dobermans, trying to get at us through the gate.

'Piss off.' was about the upshot of it.

'But you owe it to us fair and square,' said Snatch.

'Yeah, and if you can get it off me, great.'

And that was that.

*

We were sitting in 'The Feathers' early that evening when young Nobby came in smelling like the aftershave counter at Boots. And that's when I got the idea.

Ginger and I spent the evening washing out Nobby's vehicle. Then I rang Scabs and told him what we were going to do and asked him for a couple of things I had seen in his yard. He wanted to come along.

'More the merrier.' I told him.

We all met at my place early the next morning and off we went to the site. Ginger had brought some bones for the dogs in case they were loose. I had brought my shot gun for the same reason. We had a jemmy each and some boxes in the lorry. There was no one around. They had all gone off to the races.

Nobby backed up to the pond and dropped in the hose.

'Beats sucking up sewerage.' He said, as he

switched on the pump of his sludge gobbler.

He empties septic tanks, un–blocks drains that sort of thing, one man Dyno–rod that's our Nobby.

Meanwhile Ginger and Snatch caught the birds and put them into the boxes. I helped jemmy up the aviaries and we loaded them in my truck. We had plenty of time and it was a lovely sunny day, very nice for the ladies at Ascot.

When we had finished, Ginger and Snatch went to sort the birds out. They lined Ginger's garden with the new birdhouses and settled the birds in, he was well chuffed. Then they went round to Snatch's and built his kids an aviary, complete with half a dozen of Ginger's budgies.

Nobby emptied the fish into the water tanks that Scabs had brought round to my house and not one of them fish died

So, of course, I had to build a pond in my garden. Looks lovely it does, flood lights, fountain, special filter system.

I can't sleep at night sometimes. It makes me ill. Thinking that a heron could come down and eat a couple of grands' worth of fish in one go.

Of course the brothers knew it was us, but fairs fair and they owed us, status quo, see?

Ginger breeds his birds and sells them to the posh new garden centre run by the two Pikey brothers.

You have to laugh, don't you?

3

NICKED

Now, my fourth wife was unpredictable. She was a good cook though. At the time it happened her hormones were playing her up and we were going through a bad patch.

I was helping an old friend of mine called Dee, to set up a massage parlour in the town. Well, you have to sample the goods if you are a ... I hate to say it... a sleeping partner.

Deborah Flower was her name, Dee Flower.

A couple of times when the wife was slagging me off, she would say that she'd get me back but what could she do?

Well, I never took no notice. Women will say anything when they've got one on them, won't they? Anyway, she went quiet for a few days and I promised to have nothing more to do with Miss Flower.

I thought it had all passed over.

Then one Saturday night I crept up the stairs to bed and found that she had put on her best nightie and was pretending to be asleep. You can always tell you know, she didn't nag at me and she had a little smile on her fissog. You should always a worry, when a bint smiles like that.

I turned over and went to sleep.

*

Six o'clock next morning. The bedroom door was flung open so hard it came off its hinges. Frightened me to death it did.

'Wakey, wakey. Rise and shine!' A large West Indian stood in the doorway with a sledge hammer in his hands.

'Fuck off back to Glasgow will you?' I groaned and buried my head in the pillow.

'Right pal. Time ta get up. The polis is here. I expect you've got a sore heed. I heard you

were plootered in the 'Feathers' last night'
D.S. Campbell grinned at me.

'Where is she?'

'That lovely wee wifie of yours? She's in the
kitchen, making us hard working coppers a
cup of tea. Now rouse yourself. I wanta take
a wee keek at your cludgie.'

'Speak English can't you.' I said as I began to
pull my clothes on, resigned.

'Will you take a cuppa before we start?'
Campbell asked.

'Nah. Let's get on with it.'

Odds on she would have poisoned it
anyway. I followed him into the bathroom.
She had fitted me up good and proper. He
went straight to the bath and pulled the
front panel off. Then we did the whole tour,
up in the loft, under the floorboards, the lot.

Now, my house is in a nice little commuter
village, full of executives, all keeping their
chins just above the mortgage. I live in one
of the council houses. There are only six, in
a terrace, almost in the centre. I have to
admit, if they asked me nicely I would park
my lorry and most of my cars down at Mal's
yard. It's only a five minute walk.

It's not much of a view, a tipper truck.

But they never say anything to my face. They write letters in the village magazine and to the council. Meetings are held in the village hall. The only time they talk to me is if they want something. The cricket clubs' mower needs fixing. The wife's car won't start or they need towing out in the winter. And, of course they need muscle to set up the village fete every year, not to mention the 'Tug of War' competition.

Anyway, you get the picture.

They had a field day that Sunday. I've never seen so many company cars being washed or so many Labradors being walked in all my life. And there's me, cuffed to a black Glaswegian policeman, walking out to a jam sandwich. I asked if we could have the blues and two's on to please the locals.

And do you know Campbell obliged!

Just the job!

*

So there I am, sitting at a table in an interview room surrounded by coppers and my collection. I never realised I had that many shooters. Smart. There was even some that I'd forgotten I had. D.S. Campbell was there, his boss Inspector Baines, a very tasty

looking lady sergeant, I hadn't seen before
and a couple more D.S.'s I knew and some
P.C.'s, all there for the fun like.

'We having' a party Mr Baines?' I asked,
nodding at the sergeant. 'Is she the
stripper–gram?'

'Shut it.' He said and slammed a machine
gun on the table.

'What's that?'

'Machine gun innit?'

'What would you want that for?'

'It's my hobby. Every one needs a hobby.
What's yours Mr Baines? You an Eddie
Stobbart spotter?'

'Very funny, remind me to laugh sometime.
What's this?'

He put another piece on the table

'Ah! I made that one Mr Baines. Always been
creative with my hands.'

'If there was any justice, you would have
had your hands chopped off years ago.'

'I didn't know you was a Muslim Mr Baines.
Wife wear a yashmack does she?'

She bloody well ought to I thought, talk about grim, frighten the wildlife his wife would.

'What's this then?' He put a handgun in front of me.

'A colt Mr Baines, what do I get when I win? A holiday in the Barbados?'

'Holiday in Wormwood Scrubs more like. Where did you get it?'

'I do a lot of shopping' at car boot sales. Could have been in a job lot. Might have found it. Me memory's not that good.'

'You, are taking the piss.' Baines said as he put the gun back and began to rummage about in my ammunition box.

'Well. Let's see.' He carefully put something down on the table.

'Do you remember what this is?'

'Yes sir, it's a grenade. It works like this. You pull this pin out.' Which I did... ...

You've never seen a room empty so fast in all your life. Flying coppers everywhere. Jammed in the doors, under the chairs.

'And you got eight seconds before it goes off.' I said to an empty room.

After a while I went to look in the corridor.

'Hello!' I called. 'Hello.'

I poked my head under a table in the hallway. 'It's all right Mr Baines. You can come out now' I said. 'It's a dummy, for practice.' I held it out to him. 'Look, that's what the red cross is painted on the side for, I'd have thought you'd have known that.'

You should have seen his face.

Campbell put a hand on my shoulder. 'I'm right peely-wally under this black skin. You maddy skull.' He said as he took me down to the cells. 'That was a wee stoter, so it was. He grinned as he shut the door.

Different language all together Scottish, innit?

I heard Campbell laughing all the way up the corridor.

Who says the filth haven't got a sense of humour?

I got five years; possession of firearms, only did two of course.

4

TAKING THE PISS

Old plod, he does ask for it though don't he?

Me and Snatch once had a good laugh at their expense.

We took a lovely top of the range B.M.W. from the road outside the local public school. It was sports day or something. There were some sweet motors parked there, but a Beamer is always a challenge. Couldn't help ourselves, we don't normally do this sort of thing, but the idiot had left his door unlocked.

Anyway. We were cruising up the M40 towards Oxford, when the old mobile disco appeared behind us. Blue lights flashing. Siren going.

Now Snatch is a good driver. Damon Hill? ... Rubbish. If Snatch had a Dad with influence he could have been a world champion, no probs. But then, since he don't know who his Dad was...

Anyway where was I?

Being chased up the motorway by a jam sandwich. Giving him a run for his money.

Snatch was wellying it in the fast lane. I saw an exit coming up.

'Turn off here.' I shout.

So, Snatch hangs a left, straight in front of an old wrinkly, hugging the middle lane. Well, it must have startled him or his glasses steamed up or something, because he veered right... into the fast lane.

The cops ploughed right up the back of him.

Must have shunted him a mile. Serves him right. I hate people who drive in the middle lane they're a bloody nuisance.Next thing I know, we're steaming down this country lane at what seemed like ninety miles an hour with a panda car up our jacksie. I have to admit. I shut my eyes. I trust Snatch with the driving, but I can't bear to look sometimes.

'Bloody 'ell!' He shouts.

I opened my eyes and wish I hadn't bothered.

'Fuck me!' I said.

A police Sierra was coming at us, head on.

'Right.' Says Snatch looking determined and stuck his boot down on the accelerator.

'We're not in Hollywood you know.' I told him. 'You aren't James Bond. There isn't room for two cars down here!'

The mad bugger just laughed and drove straight at the cop car.

The driver must have realised he meant it. At the last minute he drove up the bank and we went past him at the speed of light, must have missed him by inches.

Snatch made a noise like a chicken and gave him the finger.

I looked back in time to see him turn over, right into the path of the panda.

'Whoops!' Snatch grinned. 'That's three of 'em down. Where to next?'

He was getting carried away.

'I think I've had enough excitement today, Snatch. Let's double back to Mal's yard and leave the car in his barn for a bit. Before I need a change of underpants.'

*

We sat on some bales of hay in the barn and watched Mal stroke the Beamer.

'Eighty grand these are. Are you gonna 'ring' it?'

We thought about it for a while. But the guy we knew who would be up for the job was having a holiday at her Majesty's pleasure and I had one or two of my own irons in the fire.

Then I got the idea.'We'll put it back!''What!' They looked at me as if I'd

lost it.'Great piss take. We'll put it back exactly where we got it. Leave the radio in, give it a good clean, just in case they dust it.'

So, that's what we did.

The best valeting job the owner has ever seen. I bet.

*

Baines and Campbell came into 'The Feathers' a few nights later.

'Your men smashed up any police cars lately, Mr Baines?' I asked.

'You taking the piss?' Baines asked.

'No Sir. Not me. As if?' Snatch choked on his pint.

5

COUNTRY PURSUITS

My Granddad was a gardener at a big house and my Gran was the housekeeper. I lived with them until I was twelve. Dad was in and out the nick and me Mum disappeared when I was four. Went off with a double-glazing salesman I think. It was from Gramps I got my respect for firearms. He loved guns. He showed me how to take his gun to pieces and clean it. He would take me with him when he helped the gamekeeper on the estate. Gramps wasn't too impressed with school.

'Never done me no good,' he would say.

He taught me all about the country. I can still name the trees and birds. On my tenth birthday Gramps gave me a gun just my size. A twenty bore, lightweight, sweet as a nut. I was like a dog with two tails.

The next day, off we went to get some rabbits.

'Now boy, you must wait until the rabbit clears the hole. You understand?' Gramps rubbed at his white whiskers. 'Follow him smooth and fire low. See?' He demonstrated.

I nodded. I'd got the gun up to my eye already. Gramps put his favourite ferret down the back door of the burrow.

The rabbit flew out of the hole. I pulled the trigger. I didn't wait.I shot Gramps' favourite ferret, coming out of the hole after the rabbit! I legged it. I've never run so fast in all my life. Gramps took my gun away... after he thumped me, fairs fair.I got it back for Christmas and a baby ferret. Elvis I called it. I never told Elvis I'd shot his Dad

Now hunting is a sport I don't hold with.

Live and let live, that's what I say. I can't see what the pleasure is in chasing furry animals over the countryside and then watching dogs rip them to bits. I've seen a few hunts in my time and let me tell you I've seen more than one fox being let out of the back of a van. Poor bugger's got no chance, so much for controlling the local fox population.

Being a lorry driver in this neck of the woods you come across them all the time. The ones that make me laugh are the "hunt supporters," mostly old women who follow in their cars.

Many is the chuckle I've had sitting up in the cab, watching these fat old dears made up to the nines. Think Barbara Cartland in tweeds, headscarves tied tight under their chins, running over ploughed fields, usually uphill, tripping over each other, just to be in at the kill. Reminds me of ancient Rome and thumbs up or down.

If you have to kill a fox, one man can do the job easy with a two–two rifle and a spotlight.

Well, as I say, they like to have a day out on their horses, thrill of the chase and that. But as far as I can see the old biddies in cars, just want the blood. Weird innit?

*

Scabs and I upset them once. We were going to pick up some cars, so we'd borrowed a grabber lorry, a flat loader with a big arm to load the motors, a bit like those things at the seaside, loads of nice prizes inside, but no way will the grabber hold on to them cuddly toys.

Very frustrating.

So, I'm driving down this country lane, when we had to stop for a couple of hounds loose in the road. The dogs must have been lost because we didn't come across the rest of them for a mile or so. Then we had to stop, because a little red Peugeot blocked the lane where two cars had parked in a gateway.

'Bloody hunt.' says Scabs. 'I've got to be back to see a bloke this afternoon.'

I hit the horn as a fat old moo got out of the Peugeot.

She pushed up her chest and shouted. 'You'll have to wait!'

'OI! Come back!' Scabs shouted as she disappeared into the field, tying on her headgear. She wasn't coming back 'til she'd seen blood.

'It's a good job Ginger isn't here.' I said. 'He'd be up there strangling the hounds with his bare hands.'

'Nah. He wouldn't hurt the dogs. But he'd be knocking a few heads together!'

The thought of it made me laugh.

I left my hand on the horn. Doubt they had

heard it over the noise of the dogs and horses and trumpets. Scabs was seriously pissed off.

'Move it,' he said.

'What, shunt it? Where to?'

'Nah!' He nodded at the field. 'Pick it up and shove it in there!'

I swung the arm out and picked the little car up. Over the hedge it went and into the field.

A short weedy looking woman ran into the road as we were about to drive away.

'You swine! You hooligans!' She held up her hands and shouted. 'Stay where you are whilst I summon the police.'

She got in her car and backed it out of the gateway and stopped in front of us. Well, what could we do? We pulled our hats down to hide our faces and got on with it.

You should have seen her face as she went over the hedge. Looked like a codfish she did. I didn't drop her. I put her down very gently. Got ourselves some sweet motors that day. We kept a couple for banger racing.

Detective Sergeant Campbell came down
'The Feathers' and questioned us about it. 'I
know you use a flat bed truck, had to be you
lot.'

'Would I do that to a lady?' I say. 'Me? The
perfect gentleman.'

Snatch butted in then and said that we'd
been at his place playing cards, with Ginger,
Bandit and Nobby.

'See you.' Campbell pointed a finger at me.
'Let me give you a wee word of advice.
Baines is out ta get yer. He's no a happy
man.' The DS drained his glass. 'He's
making my life a misery, so he is.'

'What can I say Mr Campbell?' I said.

'Ah bloody well know it was you. She was a
magistrate's wife, she'll no give up on it.'

'As much as I'd like to make Mr Baines
happy, like Snatch says we was at his place
playing cards.'

'Aye, and the eight o'clock pig from
Heathrow is just flying over.' He put his
jacket on. 'I'll be back,' he said as he turned
to leave.

'Missing you already,' I said.

D.S.Campbell gave me the finger.

It can't be easy for him. Being foreign twice over like.

6

FRIENDS

Ginger is a few years older than me. I first
met him on the towpath by the canal. Lovely
sunny day it was, so I decided on a stroll by
the water on my way to meet the lads at the
'Lock Keepers.'

I'm walking along minding my own
business, when I see this huge hairless man
by the side of the water. He had taken off
his jacket and it was in a heap next to him.
The guy had a head like a billiard ball and
he had his foot on the head of this bloke
floundering about in the water. As I got
nearer he took his foot away and let the guy
get his breath. Then he stuck his boot back

and pushed him under again.

I stood next to the bald man. The guy in the water was splashing and gurgling. We were getting soaked.

'You gonna kill him?' I asked and offered him a fag.

'Dunno.' He took a Marlborough. 'Thanks mate.'

We smoked for a bit. He pulled his boot off the geezer for a second or two. Then put it back on.

'What are you doing it for?' I asked.

He took his foot away and carefully picked up his jacket. Shivering inside it was a little puppy. It looked like a drowned rat.

'I'm only doing what he was doing to this little fella.'

'Right.' I said.

The man was trying to drag himself up onto the towpath. Gasping for breath he was and he'd nearly got out.

'Let me help.' I said and took a kick at the wet guy. Back he went into the water.

'Ginger.' Said Ginger and gave me his hand.

'Pleased ta meet you.' I said and gave him my name.

After a while we let the bugger out and politely pointed out the error of his ways, then he squelched off.

'Coming up the 'Lock Keepers'?' I said.

Ginger picked the up the puppy. 'Yeah. He could do with a brandy to warm him up.'

And that's how I met Ginger.

*

Mal, Snatch, Scabs, Bandit (he had two arms then) and me went to school together. Or not went to school together more like. We were in the same class.

Once, the rumour went round the school that if you baked banana skins till they went black and smoked them, it was like pot. It didn't work. We spent all day on it. Burnt one of Mrs Snatch's baking trays and got a clip round the ear for our troubles.

Scabs was known as 'Scabby Abby' in those days on account of his spots, a very interesting skin disease he had, sometimes it went round in circles and sometimes it went in straight lines across his chest. No one thought about the mice and hamsters he kept in cages at his house. He used to let them run across his neck and back like when he was playing with them or trying to impress girls. The girls used to scream a lot when a mouse or hammy emerged from his shirt in the classroom. He used to keep them in his haversack in one of those little cages you get at the pet shop and feed them with his lunch. Anyway when he got to about thirteen the Doctor finally worked out what the situation was and gave him some ointment and it cleared up a treat. Scabs stopped playing with rodents. He had discovered there were more interesting things he could do with the girls. But we still call him Scabs.

Snatch got his name because cars have always been his first true love. Motors have fascinated him since he got his first pedal car. He can drive anything. He got his name because as soon as he could see over a steering wheel, he just had to get behind one. And anyway Sidney is not a very good name for a getaway driver. Snatch drives a J.C.B. for a living.

I remember his first drive of a machine. He nicked it and according to his mum, God paid him back. We were about seventeen at the time and we had been to 'The Target', a pub in a village outside the town. Completely stocious we were. The money we had pooled was spent, so, no taxi.

'Best start walking.' Scabs said. 'We can thumb it.'

'Are you mad? There's no one on the road round here at this time,' I said, looking round for a likely motor to nick.

'Why don't Snatch go and get one.' Mal said and sat down in the bus shelter. 'He's been practising.'

'Ok. Don't worry lads,' said Snatch, 'You wait here and I'll be back wiv some transport.'

Ten minutes later we heard it. Five minutes after that, we saw it. He'd gone and nicked a J.C.B. We climbed up into the cab. Bit of a squash like. So Mal sat in the bucket. And off we flew. Crawled really, until Snatch got the hang of it. Then we did about fifteen miles an hour. He parked it on the big roundabout in the centre of town. I didn't see what happened exactly, since I was having a slash at the time. All I heard was Snatch saying 'Whoops.'

Which is not an unusual saying for Snatch.

'Bugger Me!' Says Scabs.

'No thanks,' says Mal.

'Oh Fuck!' Bandit said and sat down.They began to shout for me just as I arrived on the scene. Snatch was holding his right hand up. Blood everywhere. He was white as an uncooked bun.

'He had his hand in the way when we lowered the bucket for Mal to get out.' Scabs said.

'Don't it hurt?' I asked.

'Nah. Where's the top of me finger gorn?'

Well. We all looked for it. But we were a bit rushed, feeling we ought to get him up to casualty, as well as getting away before the filth arrived.

*

'Shock.' The nurse said as she stitched him up without painkillers. His finger didn't hurt till the next day.

We couldn't make the poor bugger walk home, could we?

Now, the bus station was right opposite the door to the hospital in those days. As we walked past they were washing the buses ready for the day. And there was a green double decker all gleaming and with its engine running.'God will provide,' said the poster on the wall of the Evangelist church opposite. And he had. Snatch wanted to drive but we didn't let him. Scabs took us home in style. We dropped Snatch off at his door and left the bus on the playground of the estate where we lived in them days.

We got probation.

Snatch's Mum said that God had paid him back by smiting off his fingertip. Can't see it myself, I can't see God bothering with little things like that.

Got enough on his plate I should think.

7

Uncle Bill

Ginger, Scabs, Snatch and I were sitting in Mal's barn having a planning session. We had decided to pull three jobs in the same town at the same time and take some tips from 'The Italian Job.' We couldn't fix the traffic lights but we had friends with lorries who could park or 'break down' in strategic places. Friday the market is on, banks would have wages etc. It would take a lot of planning but we were confident. We sat around with a map of the town selecting likely banks, Post Offices, building societies and thinking of who we could take with us. We needed one more heavy and another driver.

'What about Nobby?' Ginger said. 'He's always wanted to come along on a job.'

'Nah. They'd find him through his aftershave.'

I always think of Nobby as a bit of a pansy boy. Which is wrong, he can be evil and has been done for GBH. Seems he caught one of his ladies snogging a guy outside a nightclub. Nobby hit him and left an imprint of the fella on a metal garage door. I've been in a few scraps with him and he does get mad if someone wrinkles his suit or messes up his hair.

"He can park his sludge gobbler at the main traffic lights, unblock some drains." I said.

'What about Bandit?' Snatch said. 'He's strapped for cash.'

Now Bandit, on the face of it isn't a good bet for a getaway driver, him only having only one arm. I was told he lost his arm in the East End, with his own sawn off, who knows?

I, for one, am not going to ask him.

But he does have some advantages. He plans really well. Has to, don't he? Gets a car in advance, automatic of course. Adapts it to his needs. Bandit is really good with his hands. Sorry, hand. And the cops aren't going to have a one armed man spring to mind.

He's never been caught. Most of the time he works on the market selling veg. He does a bit of buying and selling on the side. He never holds on to the goods. Moves them on quick to buyers he's already lined up.

So I said okay to Bandit.

'We can't hang on to the money for too long.' I said. The Old Bill in that particular town is known for its efficiency. That's why we wanted to do it, a challenge.

'Anyone got any ideas?'

Ginger polished his head. 'I think I might. Let's have another look at that map.'

Ginger does a bit of part time work for the council, community service, 100 hours. A group of them had been tidying up a cemetery in the area we were looking at.

'See.' Ginger pointed to a place where the road split at the edge of the cemetery making a triangle. 'One road takes traffic south of the town. The other goes north. There's a high wall there right on the point. Behind that is a gap and then a tall hedge, they throw the grass cuttings behind it, compost heap like.'

'So?'

'So, we all bung the bags and the shooters over the wall. Then if we do get picked up, we're clean... Sweet innit?' Ginger grinned. 'We can pick them up later.'

'Yeah!' said Snatch. 'How about I have a hearse away? I've never driven one of those.

'Cor. That would be sweet,' said Scabs.

'Nah. Just get us three G.T.I.'s for the jobs. And something inconspicuous for picking up the money,' I told Snatch.

*

Ginger, Scabs and me were sitting in 'The Feathers' with Bandit, making the last minute arrangements when in bounced Snatch, grinning all over his face.

'Me Uncle Bill has died, he said rubbing his hands together.

We didn't know what to say. Snatch didn't seem too upset, quite the opposite.

'He's being buried on Monday!' He grinned.

'Oh,' says Ginger. 'Sorry to hear that.'

'Nah! I'm thinking of the job. Auntie Beryl wants him at home on Friday. Can't think why. She couldn't stand the old bugger when he was alive.' Snatch wiped his nose on his sleeve.

'Yeah?' I said.

'Yeah! And I am going to get him. Friday morning, in the hearse! Seems the undertaker is a distant relative of Beryl's and he wants to go to the races or something for the weekend.'

'I know where I can lay me 'ands on some black suits,' said Bandit. 'We'll need a couple more men though.'

We tossed round a few names and decided Nobby could have his chance. 'He'll look good in black.' Said Ginger.

'His work mate can do the stuff with the 'gobbler.'

So it was agreed. The hearse would be used to pick up the money. Nobby and Mal, who has a naturally miserable fissog would be in the hearse with Snatch driving. Me and Scabs would do the bank with a guy called Spud as driver. Ginger and Spud's mate, Chopper would do the building society with Bandit in the car. I had organized a couple of reliable acquaintances to do the Post Office.

'Sweet,' I said, 'let's all drink to Uncle Bill.'

Ginger got a round in and we raised our glasses. 'Good old Uncle Bill!'

*

The Friday arrived and our part went smoothly enough. We lobbed the bags over the wall and went on our way, same with the others. The town was gridlocked and plod were buzzing around like demented bees with their wings cut off.

Meanwhile Nobby and Mal, all dressed in black waited for Snatch and the hearse to turn up. It was late!

The undertaker had got called out and it took him longer than he thought calming the grieving widow. Her husband had died on the bog so she had to go next door every time she wanted a pee because she couldn't face going in her own. Which it seemed was quite often.

Anyway, while Auntie Beryl went to the shops to get stuff for the wake, they got Uncle Bill out of the coffin. He was in good nick and wearing his best suit, so they decided that he would like to go on one last job. They strapped him in one of the seats behind the driver, where the bearers sit. Nobby sat next to Bill, which he was not happy about, never having seen a stiff before, let alone having one leaning on him.

The traffic was at a stand still in town. So Snatch took a series of short cuts down the back streets. Mal said he never knew that a hearse could go so fast. Seems Nobby had to keep Uncle Bill upright as Snatch showed off his hand brake turns.

They went through the Cemetery gates on two wheels. The money and shooters went into the coffin. The hearse moved off towards the entrance and that's when they heard the police sirens. One of Joe public must have seen us lob the bags over the wall.

Snatch got to the gates at the same time as the first police car turned in. The hearse and the jam sandwich stopped, nose to nose. The lads pulled down their top hats and bowed their heads.

Then, would you believe it? The copper saluted and backed back. The guys looked as solemn as they could and drove slowly out and down the road.

*

That night, we wanted to take Uncle Bill with us to the pub. But Auntie Beryl put her foot down.

'It isn't hygienic.' She said. 'And anyway I've

spent my married life trying to get him out of the pub.' She sniffed, 'It will be the first time he's stayed at home on a Friday night since the beginning of the air raids.'

It was the best funeral I've ever been to. Slap up eats and we paid for all the booze, least we could do.

Uncle Bill's travels weren't over though. Beryl had his ashes in a box on the mantelpiece; she was going to make sure he stayed at home, some she scattered at Parkhurst.

'Nice touch,' said Ginger.Though I had my doubts about it.

Dee has a mate who is a cleaner. She does Beryl once a week. Seems one day she knocked over the box and hoovered it all up. Poor girl didn't know it was Uncle Bill. Dee had to tell her what it was. They rushed back and emptied the contents of the Hoover bag into the box while Auntie Beryl was asleep.

He always was a mixed up old bugger, was Uncle Bill.

8

SKIPPER

I had to bury my old dog, Skipper, last week. Dee had to take her down the vets. I couldn't face it.

Awkward. That's how you would describe Skipper. From the day she was born. Skipper's mum was a rough haired little Jack Rusell that Mal had bought for fucking Sharmain. Dad was a big old Rottweiler Border Collie cross, called Sultan that Mal kept at the yard. Bad tempered thing he was. Still I suppose I wouldn't be happy chained to a horsebox all day. Terrible bad breath Sultan had and that dog farted worse than me after I've had six pints of the home brew that Snatch makes in his shed.

You'd have thought Mal and Tracy would have realised the little dog had come into its first season. Them being sort of farm types.

*

When the time came for the puppies to arrive. The poor little dog tried hard. When she was completely knackered Mal took her down the vets. Cost him fifty quid it did, for a caesarean.There were two pups. One was dead, squashed flat. Seems that since the father was such a big dog, it made the pups too large for the poor little dog to give birth normally. Luckily the Vet took it upon himself to fix it so she couldn't have any more puppies. And that was how Skipper arrived in this world.

I've never seen such a funny looking dog as Skipper. When she was a week old she was as big as her Mum and had clumps of hair sticking out all over the place.

*

It was a hot summer's day when I went round to fetch Skipper. She was with her mum in a shed in the yard. It was behind the second hand 'above the ground' swimming pool Mal had acquired from somewhere for fucking Sharmain to play in.

'Best thing I ever got' he said, as we watched her run up the dung heap at the side of the pool and jump into the water. I don't know which was more evil looking, the dung heap or the water in the swimming pool, it had straw and muck floating on top of the murky green water. Anyway. Out she jumped and ran back up the heap and leapt into the water again.

'Come in,' Mal said, as he grabbed the puppy.

I followed Mal into the kitchen. I swear there were things living in that sink, things unknown to man. The Sunday lunch stuff was all over the place and this was a Wednesday.

The smell of dung and old grease was nearly too much for me and I don't have a weak stomach. I have to tell you that Dee keeps a fresh air spray handy in our house. Just for when Tracy and Mal come round.

'Tea?' Tracy said, mining for some mugs in the pile next to the sink.As we waited for the kettle to boil Tracy looked in the fridge for the milk. Obviously there wasn't any in there. So she bent down and picked up the cats bowl and poured that into the mugs.

'Come and sit in the other room.' She picked up the mugs. Mal and I followed her through the dining room into the lounge. Tracy left behind a trail of muck on the carpet as she walked.

She must have seen me looking at it.Tracy looked down at the floor.

'Oh, a bit of shit never hurt no one, did it?'

'No. Suppose not.' I said.

I can't remember what colour that carpet was. I've got a feeling it was pink. To tell the truth I avoid going into their house nowadays. I haven't got their natural immunity. See?

Mal put the pup on the rug in front of the fireplace.

'Get us some of yer 'ome made cake Tracy,' said Mal before I could say

'no thanks. I want to live a bit longer.'

I slipped most of my cake to the puppy. Then it crapped on the floor and Tracy wiped the carpet with the dishcloth. I've managed not to have anything to eat or drink out of that kitchen ever since.

*

I often took Skipper out in the lorry with me. She slept on my dressing gown in the corner of the bedroom. She even came on the boat, had her own little gravel box to pee in. Skipper was well known in the village. She would wander up to the pub in the summer to beg food from the people eating in the gardens. She spent hours at the playground on the village green with the local kids. Skipper would be sitting at the school gates in the mornings and at going home time. When she got too old to jump up into the cab herself, I left her at home with Dee. Whatever time I came home, there she was, sitting on the doorstep; nothing wrong with her hearing.

Then Skipper began to get fat and kept to her bed all day.

One morning I said to Dee. 'This is it. I think Skipper has something nasty growing in the woodshed. She definitely isn't her usual self. Will you take her to the vet's? Find out what's wrong.'

But Dee thought that since Skipper didn't appear to be in pain and was eating well, it was better to leave her be. 'Fifteen is old for a dog,' she said. 'Let's not have her pulled about. Not till it's necessary.'

I thought that made sense.

Dee would boil up chicken and give Skipper full cream milk. We had to have the skimmed, because Dee was on a diet and it's better for me. Some nights, as I sat eating my sardine salad or chewing a bit of skinless grilled chicken. I swear that dog would look at me out of the corner of her eye and smirk.

'No wonder you are so fat!' I'd say and Skipper would just wag her tail.

Then came the day it happened. Dee phoned me, I was at 'Dons place,' our favourite greasy spoon. Anyway. Dee was in a panic. Something was up with Skipper.

'Skipper wouldn't eat her porridge at breakfast.' Dee said. 'And now she won't even look at her lamb and rice...' She broke off... 'I hope you're not having a fry up there?' She sounded suspicious.

'No.' I said looking down at my ham, chips and egg.' Just the salad you put in my box.'

'You sound shifty to me. I think I'll have a word with Don about you... Oh God! ... You'd better come home quick. Skipper's laying in her basket panting and whining. She's in agony by the looks of it. I'm going to call the vet out.'

The cafe went silent when I told them the bad news. I thought Ginger was going to cry. I have to confess to having a lump in my throat as I left.

*

The Vet's car was parked outside the house when I got there.I hoped I wasn't too late. Dee opened the door. She looked as if she had been hit with a brick. I put my arms round her and asked where Skipper was.

'In the kitchen... The vet's been marvellous... I'm so glad I rang him.' Dee looked worn out.

The kitchen was very quiet as I opened the door. I have to admit I was shaking. The Vet was kneeling over the dog basket in the corner of the kitchen. He looked up at me with a serious look on his face. He seemed very young for a vet.

'Mother and babies are doing fine' he grinned. 'See?'

He stood up and there was Skipper lying on her side suckling five pups. And we had thought the old dog was past it! Got the menopause. I had to sit down. Tears ran down my face, only because Dee had burst out balling.

Off went the young vet, with a case of whisky and a box of cigars in his boot. Dee and I just sat there, in the kitchen, staring at Skipper and her pups. Then the phone started to ring. It rang all day, everyone asking after Skipper. People banging on the door, some brought bones, some even gave us flowers.

I said to Dee. 'We ought to put bulletins up on the gate. Like they do at the palace!'

The lady that walks blind dogs gave us a proper bed thing with special white bedding for pups and a wooden playpen. People who knew about these things brought bundles of newspapers!

Skipper was the talk of the village.

Folk still talk about that day. Everyone wanted a puppy. My son Spider had one. The other four went to some very posh homes in the village. I often see these strange hairy dogs walking round the lanes. We never found out who the father was. Though I have my suspicions.

9

FAIR'S FAIR

Now, Snatch don't have much luck. So when
Scabs had this Japanese People Carrier come
into the yard. We thought of Snatch and all
those kids. It was an insurance write-off
after being in a prang. The chassis was a bit
twisted. Well if they won't buy British, what
do people expect? Mal spent some time on
the motor and it looked sweet though it
gave you a weird feeling when you drove it.
It was like driving a shopping trolley.

But Snatch was real proud of it. Mandy
drove the people wagon most of the time.
She looked like the woman in the shoe. All
these little faces, staring, cross-eyed, out

the window. Sardines spring to mind. Ginger
called it the nutty bus. And I have to
confess, it did look a bit like the mini coach
that picks up the 'special kids' in the
mornings, to take them to their special
school.

And Mandy, well, she isn't all there herself
really. She takes slimming pills so she won't
get fat. Well, you do get fat when you're up
the duff don't you? She drinks gin and
throws herself down the stairs. But them
babies just stick with her whatever she
does. Anyway, Snatch arranged to pick us
up and buy us a pint in 'The Feathers,' as a
thank you.

It was gleaming. The car smelt a bit funny.
Apparently the baby had got the squits. We
left 'The Feathers' after an hour or so.
Ginger walked out with Snatch, Scabs, Mal
and me bringing up the rear.

'Oh my God!' shrieked Snatch. Ginger
propped him up.

'I spent ages spraying that.' Mal looked
upset. 'I bet the paint isn't even bloody well
dry yet.'

Some bastard had turned into the space
next to the kid-mobile and hadn't judged it
properly. We were looking at a twelve-inch
long dent, with white paint left on the

scratches.

I thought Snatch was going to burst into tears.

'Look.' said Scabs.

Backed into the space opposite was a white Ford Escort van.It had a dent on the wing which was covered in blue paint.

'I'm going in there to give him a slap.' Snatch headed back to the pub.

We caught hold of him.

'Come on, you can't go storming in there.' I said. 'We'll play this a bit clever. I'll go in. You stay out here.'

I knew who owned the white van. His name was Russell. Not a nice man.

'Was that you?' I asked him politely. 'Who caught the side of my car? In the car park just now.'

'No mate. Not me.'

'Come on.' I said 'Your wing is covered in blue paint.'

'Not yours, pal. I did that this morning. Didn't I Jon?' He smirked at the large gorilla sitting next to him.

'Yeah.' Said the ape standing up. 'He did. Want to make something of it?'

'Nah. If you say it weren't you. That's fine.'

I heard them laughing as I walked through the bar.

Now I like a laugh as much as the next man. But I hate being laughed at. Russell has a builders yard, I bought some red seconds from him once. The bricks he delivered were crap and half of them were yellow. He gave me some more but they were crap too. By the time I had sorted them and found some more. I reckon I was down a couple of hundred smackers.

'Don't worry Snatch my dear.' I said. 'Russell won't get away with it. I've got an idea.' And I did. 'Let's go back to my place.'

My tipper was parked outside my house. We climbed up into the cab. 'Observe.' I said. 'My tipper is full to the brim with hard core. I need to find somewhere to dump it and the very place has sprung to mind.'

*

Russell had a very nice house on the main road, just before the turning to his yard. The drive is three cars wide and that night we could see it had been newly tarmacked, done good job too. Right in the middle of the drive stood his shiny black Mercedes sport, only two months old, complete with poser plate ... RUS 11. The house was in darkness. I let Snatch do it.

'Whoops!' Snatch said as he dropped the lot, right on top of Russell's car

Sweet.

10

THE EVILS OF DRINK

Now, drink has got me into trouble a few times I can tell you.

And I do drink a lot. It's in my genes. I married my third wife when I was on a bender. I don't know how it happened. One morning I woke up and there she was. Couldn't even remember her name.

You've heard the song, of course. "I've never been to bed with an ugly woman, but I've sure woken up with a few." I married mine! Only lasted six months, I still can't remember her name.

It was drink that ruined my first smart suit.

The place to go drinking for us young'uns was 'The Target' across town. The landlord wasn't too fussy about the age limit. I'd polished my best shoes, put my new suit on and didn't I look the business? Off I went on the bus with Snatch.

Great. At about ten o'clock, the girls we had been chatting up all evening, disappeared into the bog. Did a runner, didn't they? Climbed out of the window. Can't thing why. We kept them well topped up with Babycham all night.

Scrubbers.

We decided to drown our sorrows over a game of pool. I began to drink Bacardi and Lucosade. Slipped down a treat. The last bus had long gone so Snatch rang for a taxi that refused to come out. They all did.

'Let's walk.' I said, being young and fit. 'We can go across country.' I said. 'It'll be quicker.'

Snatch thought the road would be quicker so we agreed to meet at his house and see who was right. I vaguely remember climbing over the first stile as Snatch wove his way down the lane.

*

I got the story a couple of days later. Mostly from an old copper called Jock, who was in charge of the cells in them days.

Seems Snatch fell down a hole in the road. This convinced him there were wild animals about. Well, it would, wouldn't it? Logical. He had been watching Tarzan and because he was totally inebriated Snatch assumed he'd dropped into an animal trap. He never thought 'road works.' He thought 'great white hunters.'

Snatch eventually managed to climb out of the hole and then legged it... up the nearest tree.

Which happened to be a very nice cherry belonging to the Mayor. Good old Snatch, he got nearly to the top but missed his footing, tried to hang on with his right ear until he slipped back down to the first branch.

Woke up the whole house.

The Mayor came down in his pyjamas. He got hold of Snatch's leg and pulled. Snatch wasn't having any of it. Thought it was a Python or something. He squealed like a stuck pig and made a fight of it.

Snatch was not coming out of that tree.

When the cops got there. The mayor was

swinging on Snatch's ankles and blood from Snatch's ear was pouring over his new striped pyjamas, the Mayor's that is, Snatch wasn't wearing any as he had been in the pub with me.

The Mayor's wife, in her best flannelette nightie and fluffy slippers was hanging on to the Mayor's knees, in case he disappeared into the tree to be eaten by whatever it was that had made a start on him.

Anyway. They sewed Snatches ear back on in casualty.

*

Meanwhile, I had crossed the first field, which had been newly ploughed. Then I hit the barbed wire. I was aiming for the field gate. I went back and tried again but rebounded off the wire on the other side.

'Sod yer.' I said to the gate. 'If you're going to keep moving, I'll climb over the wire.' And I did. When I got half way across the next field I came over all sleepy. So I decided to lie down and have a little kip.

*

I was nudged awake by a black wet nose. I

pushed it away. Then it snorted steam at me. Surrounded by bullocks I was. 'Bloody 'ell.' I shouted and jumped up. The cows skidded away and I held onto my head till the world stopped spinning. I had no idea where I was and my head was thumping.

Slowly, very slowly I walked towards the field gate. Down the lane I went, until I saw a bus shelter. I sat there until the first bus arrived, wondering if I'd got a brain tumour.

'Where you going?' The bus conductor stared at me.

'Where does this bus go?' I said it very carefully because my mouth wasn't working proper.

'Town.' He said not taking his eyes off me.

'Then that's where I'm going.' The bus got surprisingly full. People going off to work for the early shift. No one sat next to me on the bench seat near the door and they didn't half give me some funny looks.

Impressed by my new suit perhaps?

Now this particular village, Street End, where I ended up, is well known for interbreeding. They are all wanting in the head. They've got crossed eyes, wear knitted bobble hats and wellies all year round. So, I didn't take too much notice of them. I was a stranger. I could have landed from Mars.

*

I got off the bus in town, walked round to Snatch's place and went into the kitchen through the back door.

'Bloody 'ell! What ever's happened to you!' His mum said and began to pick up the bits of the cup she'd just dropped.

'What do you mean? This is me new suit innit? Smart eh?'

Mrs Snatch grabbed my ear and marched me into the hall. She shoved me in front of the mirror. My new suit was torn and covered in grass stains. My face was a mass of cuts and grazes. Mud had dried over my shoes and trouser legs. My eyes were a lovely shade of yellow and red.

'Sidney! Move yer arse.' Mrs Snatch shrieked up the stairs.

Deafened me in one ear she did. Snatch, dressed only in his underpants, his ear all bandaged up, wandered to the top of the stairs rubbing his eyes. Not a pretty sight.

'Whoops.' He said when he saw me.

'Get this bloody mate of yours into the bath

and give him some of your clothes to wear.'
She wrinkled up her nose. 'Pooh! You don't
'arf niff.'

Half an hour later I had my knees under the
kitchen table, tucking into a cooked
breakfast. Dressed in clothes two sizes too
small.

Mandy stuck her head round the door.'We're
going to the flicks tonight

Snatch. Don't forget... Bleedin 'ell! What
happened to you two then?'

'I wish people wouldn't keep asking me
that.' I said, 'I was just very tired last night
and went to sleep in a field and Sidney here
had a fight with a tree.'

'Oooh. Touchy ain't we?' Mandy said and she
wiggled off down the path.

Mandy and Snatch had been courting since
she was fourteen. So she must have been
about sixteen then. How women do change,
it's uncanny.In them days Mandy was all

blonde beehive and high heels. Nice little
figure she had then. She worked in a hair
dressers and smelled of 'Twink.'

The women in those days used to plaster
their faces with this stuff called 'pan-stick.'
They had white faces with black eyes, like

Pandas. When you got to grips with a bit of skirt, bits would come off it in your hands. Hairpieces, eye lashes, nails. They had things called roll-ons that squeezed their bellies in. When you got a bit of totty home and it had taken all it's bits off and it's stomach had got out, it could turn you right off. Now, of course it's the natural look. They don't know how lucky they are, these young'uns. At least what you see is what you get.

*

Now back to the drink, which was where I started out. Drink got me six months. Suspended. It was my birthday and so at some point in the evening I decided to have a shot of each optic gathered together in a pint pot.

I have to say that after I threw up I felt much better.

I'd been banned from the local, so we were drinking in the "Green Door" in the village down the road. It was only a mile away. Jim, the landlord kept a good cellar, the beer was cheap and he was never fussy about closing times. Being banned from the local village pub was no loss, it was run by a couple of ex teachers who didn't like beer drinkers. What they really wanted was a restaurant. I bicycled down to the 'Green Door' on account of my licence had been suspended for six months. But I walked back.

Uphill innit?

When I got back to the village I realised I hadn't got any fags. Panic. I had to pass the village shop on the way to my house; they sold fags. Not open. Well, it was two in the morning. The house next door was having an extension built. So I fetched a brick and bunged it through the shop window. Picked up forty Marlborough's and went home to bed. I left a tenner on the counter.

Next day. My boy Paul went round and asked for the change. The shopkeeper wasn't amused. He rang the filth.

He had no sense of humour that man.

11

Public transport

Snatch has got a brother called Des, who is ten months younger than him. He's a sandwich short of a picnic. We used Des once on a job, just the once. Snatch had got the flu. The whole family had got it. They only had two sprogs then and one on the way, as usual. They must keep a bed especially for Mandy up the maternity home.

Anyway, when I called round to see if Snatch was up to the job, he looked awful. Mandy looked worse. She began pushing the Hoover round.

'Don't go doing that Mand.' says Snatch all concerned. She switched it off and smiled at him

'Do it when I'm not here.'

'Sod off!' Mandy says and slammed the door on her way out.

That made me laugh.

I heard him say another good one once. It was in the summer. We were sitting on his step with a couple of cans when Mandy, who was about ten months pregnant by the look of her, came out with two big black bags of rubbish. She headed up the path towards the dustbins. Snatch shouts.

'Don't carry them great big heavy bags Mand.'

She stops and turns to look at us. How thoughtful I think to myself.

'Take them one at a time.' Snatch called.

And she did. She's a silly cow.Where was I? Oh yeah. Des. Well, Snatch was indisposed so I thought I'd give Des a chance. If he was half as good a driver as Snatch he'd do O.K.Des picked me and Scabs up at a bit of waste ground by the trading estate. He hadn't picked the best of cars. Still, a Lada doesn't get noticed does it? But apparently the owner had left the keys in it and "beggars can't be choosers" as they say. We checked it had petrol and that we had our balaclavas and then sat in the back with our sawn-off shotguns.

We were doing the sub-post office at Street End. It all went sweet until we ran outside.

There was no one in the car. Scabs tried the door. 'Fuck!'It was locked.We didn't hang round to find out where Desmond had gone.Down the road we legged it, each of us carrying a sports bag full of pension money.

'Look.' shouts Scabs pulling off his balaclava. 'A number 26.' He kissed the air. 'Thank you God.'

We jumped on board just as it pulled out and went upstairs. Well, we needed a fag. No smoking on the bottom deck. Collapsed in the back seat I caught my breath and shoved the shooters in the bags. I take it back. Everything I've ever said about public transport. The conductor even changed a ten-pound note for us.

I bet you think we are the only people to make a getaway in a double decker. But I do know of someone else, I'll tell you about him later. When we finally caught up with Des we got the story. Seems he got peckish and went round the corner to the chippy. He was just coming back when he saw us disappear onto the bus. I used all my self-restraint and didn't give him a slap, nor did he get any money.

*

A few months later, we were walking through the town on a Saturday afternoon, packed with people it was. I hate Saturday shopping. Come to think of it, I hate shopping. Scabs dug me in the ribs and pointed. The traffic was going dead slow and stop. We watched as this real sweet red B.M.W. 635csi was stopped at the traffic lights. It's washer /wipers were going overtime. Poor bugger inside must have put them on and couldn't turn them off. How embarrassing, it was making a terrible noise and every one was gawping at it.

'Should take the fuse out.' Scabs said.

Then through the white foam, every second or so, we saw Des looking desperate as the car slowly got covered in bubbles. We laughed till we bust. Why drive a hot car like that through the town beats me.Des became a butcher. Well, he works in the bacon factory. Packing. Just as well really.

12

AMATEURS

Now down the road from Nobby lived a bloke called Bob Banks. Reckoned himself a bit of a poet. Too much of the old wacky baccy, if you ask me, bit of a hippie, away with the fairies most of the time. One day a letter came for Bob with a giro inside. He'd claimed for something... anyway. There was a typing mistake on it. It was addressed to Mr Rob Banks. I don't know if he'd had magic mushrooms for breakfast or something? But the silly bugger thought it was a message from God.

You know... Go forth and rob some banks.

Well. Bob came round and told me all this. Apparently someone had suggested that he should ask me if he could come with us on our next job.

I said no.

Bob says 'it's all right, because God will be on our side.'

I said no again, but I told him to wear one of his Mum's support stockings over his head if he was going to try his hand. He asked to borrow a shooter.

I said no.Though I did wish him luck. I don't know how he did it.I don't really want to think about it.Fluke.

A week later, Bob grinning like the proverbial, put a bag of money on my kitchen table. 'I left the other bag on the bus.' He said.

'What? You lost half your takings? On a bus!'

I told you I knew of someone else who had made a getaway on a bus.

'What do I do now?' He said. 'I seen a film once where all the notes was marked. So the fella got caught.'

Films? Fiction! Well, what could I say, except. 'Leave it to me. I'll sort it out for you.'

'I want you to give it to Green Peace,' he said.

'No problem.' I told him.

If he thought I was going to hand over a load of cash to some hand knitted, fish loving, crack pots. He was madder than them.

Poor old Bob, he did it again.

He got nicked, of course. The Judge didn't swallow the God thing. Bob got put away for treatment. The last I heard of him he was up a tree somewhere, protesting.

13

PERVERTS

Now what people do in private is their own business. Shirt lifters are all right, as long as they don't touch me. You get a few inside like. But the panty wasters never tried it on. Didn't fancy me, maybe?

Knew they'd get their heads kicked in more like.

The child molesters, they get separated inside. Just as well or there'd be a blood bath but occasionally you can get hold of one. The screws hate them too and sometimes are prepared to look the other way. Best thing the law could do is cut their balls off first offence and top them on the second, I say. But Dee has a better idea. She says the most effective thing would be to lock them in a room full of mothers. Horrible thought.

*

Some time back, a flasher arrived at the village I live in, he was seen by the fence at the back of the village Primary School. Then he was in the kids' area on the village playing field and he started lurking in the woods that surround the village, popping out at ladies walking their dogs and kids on ponies. I have to say. I can't understand them horsey lot. They let their kids out on animals, when the little mites aren't even old enough to ride a bike safely down the road.

Anyway, me and Mal were sitting in "The Feathers" talking about the flasher.

'He could leap out at Tracy, she exercises her horses in the woods sometimes.' Mal said.

'Not unless he's bloody barking mad.'

'Well fucking Sharmain goes through them woods.' Mal drained his pint. 'In this weather a lot of the kids play there and it's the holidays, coming up?' He banged down his pint pot. 'If I catch 'im I'll kick his balls in.'

'You know. That's not a bad idea.' I got up and reached for the glasses. 'He needs a slap.'

'What?'

'Give him a kicking, Mal. We could get someone to walk through the

woods, follow behind.'I toddled off to the bar and came back with a couple of grouse.

'Who will we get to do it? Tracy?'

'No, I told you, no one's going to jump out at her Mal. You don't get many flashers with white sticks, do you?'

'Well I ain't sending fucking Sharmain. No way. What about Mandy?'

'She's due to drop any minute. We don't want to end up delivering' babies. No. I was thinking of Dee. She's game for most things and being so short, she could be taken for a kid.'

'Yeah.' Mal leered and he licked his lips.

'Yeah.' I knocked back the whisky in one. 'Come on. Let's get the lads.' and we went up to the massage parlour that Dee owned.'

*

In the event it was third time lucky. Dee had
Mal's little Jack Russell on a lead. Scabs
wanted her to take one of his Rottweiler's
but I thought it might just put the perv off.
It would be a brave man, showing his todger
to them dogs. They might think it was
lunch.

The four of us followed, dressed in our
working gear; black clothes, with black
balaclavas, doing' our impression of S.A.S.
men in the jungle. Dee disappeared round a
corner in the path.

We heard her say in a very loud voice. 'My
God! Is that it? I've seen bigger ones in the
playgroup! I'd put it away if I were you.
There might be a hungry bird about.'

She might be tiny, but she can be scary. I
call her "the Sergeant Major."

So off we charge.

'Whoops.'

Snatch falls over... ... of course. And there
he was, the flasher, a small pale, red headed
weasel-like bloke, playing with his little
white Percy. He saw us, turned and ran. Dee
let go of the dog. It grabbed his trouser leg
and tripped him up. We politely told him not
to come back. He didn't say much. Well his

teeth had come out for a start, he just sort of groaned.

*

There are a lot of funny people in the army.Ginger says once you've been in the army, doing time is a doddle. Public schoolboys don't have a problem with the nick either. Well, you have to get something for the cost of your education, don't you? Anyway. Ginger had a great time in the army, he told us some stories.

If you were a Chutney ferret you got your bum singed. The usual, petrol down the latrine trench when said man is taking a dump and throw in a match. Little pranks like that.

One time, when Ginger's lot were billeted in Nissan huts. You know? Them tin things in a half moon shape? Ginger and his mates got seriously peeved.

It seems that some guy came along every night about one o'clock and took a slash on their hut. He couldn't be bothered to walk all the way down to the bog block. Night after night they were woken by the noise of his water hitting the metal at high pressure. By the time they got themselves out of bed and went outside. He'd gone. Now, that is perverted, to piss on your mates' house innit?

But Ginger got an idea. That night they plugged the Nissan hut into the mains electric supply and went off to sleep. They were woken by screams of agony.

When the phantom pisser came out of sickbay he had a new nickname, Sparky! You gotta laugh.

14

THE CAFÉ

There's this transport cafe that was called Donna's Place. I've been going there for years. Since I began on the lorries. When I first started to go to the cafe it was run by a girl called Donna. She had really short hair and always wore jeans. She had a mean little face, a pointy nose and rat features. Not very enticing, if you know what I mean.

But... She made the best egg and bacon sarnies you ever tasted, did Donna, with the yolks all runny and lots of ketchup. Then her friend Kath came to work with her.

Now Kath was seriously 'woof, woof.'

She must have arrived about six months
after I started calling in at Donna's place.
Seems Kath had left her husband and two
kids. Didn't think nothing of it, happens all
the time. Kath looked like a china doll, big
round blue eyes with long black lashes and
a little red mouth. Nice figure. She wore
frilly little things, all frothy, like candy floss.
We all tried to chat her up. Even Mal said
he'd like to give her one. Worth risking what
Tracy would do to him if she found out, he
said. That ought to tell you how fit she was.

But no, it wasn't to be.

Donna and Kath lived over the shop and it
was hard work for two women. But they kept
smiling. Still do. Two or three months after
Kath moved in we began to notice a change
in Donna. She took to wearing men's shirts.
Lots of women do that, I hear you say. So
what?

Then she started to wear men's trousers and
smoking 'roll ups'. After that it was cowboy
boots. The same as mine they were! Her hair
got shorter. Her voice got deeper.We tried
not to notice. Then her chest disappeared
and turned into an Adams apple.

We would see them down the pub on a
Friday night, Donna sinking pints and

smoking roll-ups. Kath sipping something with a cherry in it.

Then one day Donna told us we had to call her Don. We started running a book. Will she/he be going in for the op?

Scabs reckoned it's easy to lop the old man off, but more of a miracle to sew a todger on. You never know though, the wonders of modern science and all that.

They still run the cafe, only now it's called Don's Place. We call it Don's Dynamic DinerNone of us We just treat Don as one of the boys. What else can you do? They still make the best bacon and egg sarnies for miles!

15

COALTAR SOAP

I have been living here since I left my first wife. I won't tell you the name of the village. Don't need to know that. Do you? The council had to house me because I had custody of the kids. She was a fruit cake my first wife. It runs in the family. A good thing we didn't have any girls.

I married my first wife because she was up the stick and I wanted to get away from home. I'd never met her Mum. If I had, I'd have got on the first train out... to anywhere.

We had to live at her mum's house. She had room because her old man had given up the struggle to live years before and gone to join the choir invisible. The Gran lived there too. She must have been eighty something. She had lost it completely.

Now, my first wife… Iris! That was her name. I knew it would come back to me. She had this thing about germs. It started after she had the baby.

My eldest boy is called Spider, from the minute he could move he went upwards, like Spiderman. He works on scaffolding now. High as you like he just don't care. It got worse after the second baby, Paul, was born.

If I felt a bit randy I'd have to have a shave and a bath first. She would have dipped the old man in disinfectant given the chance. Good old Iris, should have had shares in Harpic.If I went in the washing basket to get some clean socks or some one did her a favour by getting in the washing when it was raining, she would wash the whole lot again. I can see her now in her pink rubber gloves and cross over apron. Washing the steps and path in Jeyes fluid.

Gives me the shudders.

I always knew when Iris had been in a room.

Wrights coal tar! It was the only soap she would buy. She burnt it in special burners all over the house. She washed her hair in the shampoo, dabbed it behind her ears I expect. Iris had grudges, against everyone and everything, grudges that went back years. She took to writing anonymous poison pen letters when she got older, of course the family knew who it was and passed them round for everybody to read. Her other hobbies were being ill and being hard done by, at one time she sent letters to the Queen and the Prime Minister, telling them what to do in relation to "The Sex Pistols". It was something to do with washing their mouths out with soap and water and scrubbing their bollocks with bleach.

Poor Iris; how she struggled to keep her chin just below water.

I once gave her a cross and nails for her birthday but she didn't get it. No sense of humour.

My son Paul takes after me. He works down the market now. I knew he was a chip off the old block early on. I remember the day it became clear to me that I had to leave and take the kids with me.

It was the first morning in two weeks that Gran hadn't poohed in her shoes that Auntie May fell face first into her porridge. May was Gran's sister and Iris had asked her to come and live with us. Reckoned she was worth a bit.

Wrong.

Anyway, we were all sitting at the kitchen table, having our breakfast. May's head dropped straight into her porridge bowl

'She's drowning' I said, panicking a bit.

Iris reached out with a pink marigold (she had got to the stage where she never took them off) and grabbed May's head by her hair and lifted her it up.

'Breathing.' Iris sniffed and dropped the old lady's head back in her porridge.

'Iris!' I said. 'The porridge!'

'Oh. It's all right. I'll give it to Mum.'

'No. You silly cow, the old git is drowning.'

Iris reached over and picked May's head up again. This time she dropped it on the table, next to the bowl.

'Just look at the mess.' She said.

'Aren't you going to call an ambulance?' I

said.

'I will. When I've cleaned up. Drag her to the door then they won't have to come in the house.'

Paul came in the back door. 'I've fed Spider. When's he coming out of the tree do you reckon Dad? He looked at his Auntie May. What's up with her?'

I prodded Paul with my fork. 'He'll probably come down in the Autumn with the leaves.' I said 'Go and ring 999.'

He shoved a bit of toast in his mouth and went into the hall. His mother gave him a cloth soaked in disinfectant to wipe the phone with. 'Before and after.' She told him. Since I did not want to be bleached or disinfected I sat half way up the stairs and studied the sports pages. Outside I could hear the noise of the ladder scraping on the wall. It was gutter-bleaching day. Door handles and coat hangers came next.

Paul sat on the bottom step reading a comic, ready to tell the ambulance men to take their shoes off when they came in.

I heard Gran shuffle up the passageway. The old lady peered at Paul who leaned back from the dragon breath.

'Who are you?' She had chocolate spread all round her mouth and down her front where she'd wiped her hands. The odd cornflake clung to her hair and she had two-day old lentil soup crusted up her nose.

'It's me Gran, Paul.'

'Where's me teeth?' She whined.

'Mum took them off you. Remember? When you bit the postman.'

'I'm old. I'll starve. Where am I?'

'Tell you what,' says Paul. 'If you give me a tenner I'll go and get them for you.'

She narrowed her little eyes, 'Two!'

'Eight!'

'Four!'

'Six!'

'A fiver and that's my last offer.'

'Okay.'

Paul held his hand out. 'Up front, and if you tell Mum where you got them. I'll pinch them back in the night.'

That's my boy, I thought.

'Shyster.' She mumbled and groped about under her skirt. The old lady handed over a screwed up note.

Paul took it. Gran snatched the fiver back and peeled out an old sweet which she shoved it into her mouth. Paul took the note back carefully between his finger and thumb. I heard Paul go into the downstairs lavvy and lift the cistern. He came out and gave the old lady her teeth.

'You'd better go out Gran. I heard Mum say she was going to hose you down in the yard today. It's Wednesday. She was looking for you yesterday.' He always was a thoughtful boy. The old lady scarpered off and then the doorbell rang. I picked up the paper and

I Then I saw it, a mobile home available for six month let.

Iris was going behind the ambulance men wiping everything they touched. She wiped Paul. And that was it. I'd had enough. I put Paul in the car and went into the back garden to fetch Spider out of the tree he was living in.

We never went back.

It didn't take the council too long to house us. I've been here ever since. But the smell of Wrights coal tar still makes me feel quite sick.

16

RELIGION

God gets about a bit. 'Specially in the village
I live in. Perhaps because it's built on top of
a hill, nearer to heaven like. After he told
Bob Banks to go forth and rob banks, God
had a Tupperware party.

There are these three old biddies in the
village. Two of them are widows. Their
husbands lost the will to live early on, I
reckon. The other is a spinster. The three of
them have always been God botherers, did
the flowers and polishing at the village
church. Every Sunday they would pass my
house all dressed up, hats and gloves, shiny
shoes. Handbags held tight under their
arms.

Anyway, God spoke to them. I'm not sure if

he chatted to them separately or all together. It was the talk of the village. They started shouting Halleluiah in the middle of the sermons and rolling about in the aisles speaking in tongues. Well, they were speaking in something foreign, anyway.I very nearly went to church to see it for myself.In the end seems the Vicar asked them not to go to Church any more. That didn't go down well I can tell you.I call them The Holy Trinity.You have to get a picture of them in your mind. I just saw them walk past. They are three seriously ugly women walking about in the rain doing good works. The two widows were dressed in yellow plastic macs with matching hats that make them look even paler than they are.Flitting about behind them, in a white plastic cloak was the one I think of as the ghost. She's the Miss. Her black wellingtons flapping round her stick insect legs. She drags this spaniel behind her wherever she goes. Soaked to the skin it was, when I saw them striding down the road, and looking distinctly pissed off.

The holy ghost was wearing a fold up rain hat tied tightly under a chin that you could cut meat with. She could have a moustache like mine if she didn't shave and her thin, hooked nose is large and always red on the end.

The tallest of the three has got stringy
straight hair. More salt than pepper. Her
face looks like a large lump of dough some
kid has tried to turn into a face. Two beady
currant eyes lurk in the folds of dough.

The middle one has got a face like a frying
pan, with pale bulging eyes. She has her
hair scragged back into a bun.

Anyway, these three women roam round the
village handing out religious texts. If
someone is having a hard time, they flock
round like vultures picking bones and read
the Bible at the poor bugger. When Dee
moved in with me, the Holy Trinity had a
field day. We were bombarded with
pamphlets and they would preach at Dee
when she went up the shop.

Living in sin. See?

I am not getting married no more. Five
times is enough.

The Holy Trinity love it when some villager
runs off with another one's wife or husband.
Really, they are obsessed with sex... other
people's sex, of course.One Monday they
stuck notices up all over the village, inviting
everyone to a Tupperware party at the holy
ghost's house.

Dee went, just to wind them up like. No one else turned up apart from the lady who sold the Tupperware. The woman looked terrified, she had never done a party for God before, apparently he had asked the trinity to organise it on his behalf. Dee came home stuffed with egg sandwiches and tea.

Then a week later the Holy Trinity trouped round with a bag, more of a sack, full of Tupperware.

She's too soft for her own good is my Dee.

17

SAILING

I had a boat for a long time.

It was a sailing boat. A catamaran. The 'Lady Day' she was called, moored near Southampton. There was this cash I had, couldn't put it in the bank, could I? Just got it out of one. Off I toddled to night classes in navigation.

I took my second wife once. She was a good cook and cleaned up, but she didn't have sea legs. Shame she didn't have any vocal chords. She moaned all the time, no telly, too cramped and she couldn't see why we didn't switch the engine on. In a sailing boat? Sacrilege innit?

The final straw came when we were going into St Malo in a gale and had to tack for at least two hours to get into port.

'If you'd switch that bloody engine on it'd only take ten minutes.' If she said it once... Ginger and Scabs had to hold me back. That was the last time she came. Most times it was me, Ginger and Scabs.

We had great times on that boat.

One night we sailed into Poole harbour. The tide was at its highest. We got a great mooring on the quay. As soon as the boat was made fast we legged it to the pub across the road. Well, we got wrecked, didn't we? Rolled into bed in the early hours. Now I sleep in the buff, so, I took off my clothes, fell back on my bunk and passed out into the land of nod.

It could have been the sun that woke me up, shining down on me through the glass roof. Or it could have been the noise of the gulls. Or perhaps it was the people. The tide had gone out in the night. The boat had sunk down below the quay. There was me, laying everything akimbo, stark naked. Up above me people were looking over shouting to their friends to, "come and look at this!" Not a good way to wake up.

Gave the holidaymakers a laugh though. It gave Scabs and Ginger something to make jokes about too.

*

One time when we were going to France, stocking up on booze and fags. Nobby asked if he could come with us. An extra pair of hands was always welcome. We used to supply some pubs and clubs and we had a big order. So I arranged a time and place for Scabs to meet us up the English coast when we got back; not a good thing to do, moor up somewhere public and load up a van with duty free.

Can't tell you where it is that we unload, suffice it to say it's convenient for lots of people and some of them aren't nice, get the picture? Best to pretend they're invisible, health wise.When we picked up Nobby. Out he came looking like a young Clarke Gable. He asked if his Granddad could come with us.

The old man was a bit down, on account of his old lady had thrown him out. Which was a regular occurrence, but this time she was really pissed off because he had set the bed on fire with his pipe and burnt the house down. He was in the Merchant Navy and I've never seen him without a pipe in his gob. He has a glass eye, which he takes out 'at the drop of a hat'. Which is why we call him Popeye.

Off we went and had a good crossing. The French port was chocca when we had arrived so we had to moor up to another boat that was moored to a buoy in the harbour.

That night we got fed up of drinking French beer. Gnats' piss, innit? So we had some brandy and went on to drink quite a bit of Chartreuse. Popeye suggested Absinthe, which apparently was the favourite tipple of French artists. Having imbibed three glasses of the stuff, I now know why their paintings are incomprehensible.

I woke up on the boat with a mouth that belonged to some one else. The sound of the kettle being filled and the gas lighting was like music from heaven. First rule of sailing, first one up makes the tea. Second rule, fresh water is limited on a boat, don't waste it.

'Great,' groaned Scabs from the bunk below. 'I'm parched'

We waited for our tea. Nothing. Slooshy noises but no tea.We crawled to the galley. Ginger had got there before us. He had Nobby in a bear hug from behind. The

bugger had been washing his hair! Covered
in suds his head was. Ginger lifted Nobby
off his feet. Marched him on deck and threw
him over.

'Bloody well rinse it in there!' Ginger shouts.

Popeye nearly pissed himself laughing.
Nobby wasn't best pleased. He had his
Calvin Klein jeans on. Funny bloke Nobby,
he spends a fortune on designer wear and
aftershave.

Still, if I drove a sewerage truck I'd be
particular, I expect.

As we started getting ready to go shopping.
Popeye asked what he could do. I told him
to put the outboard engine onto the dinghy.
He's a little old chap but he's strong. He
hefted the engine to the side of the boat.
We were getting on with what we were doing
when I heard this 'Aaaargh' sound.

There was the old man, one foot on our
boat, one on the dinghy, the outboard in his
hands. The boats were being pushed apart
as he did the splits.

Then sploosh.

In he went, nothing but a load of bubbles on
the surface.

Ginger fetched the boat hook and we scraped around. Still the bubbles came up. The boat hook caught onto something and we pulled. He was bloody heavy for a little old wrinkly. It took three of us to haul.

Then out it came.

The engine!Popeye spluttered to the surface behind it.

'You stupid old bugger.' shouts Nobby. 'Why didn't you let go of the engine.'

Popeye went under again.

When he came up, he blew water out of his pipe and said. 'What! The engine is worth more than me innit?'

I must say he did have a point.

*

I used to like sailing up to Dittisham and Noss Mayo, very picturesque and restful. If I ever really retire I shall have another boat. Can't see Dee on a boat though. Deck shoes don't have stilettos.

One year Nobby went off to one of these club holidays on the Costa del fish and chips. He came back with this bright yellow tea shirt with a palm tree on it and the name of the place printed below. He was wearing it when we sat out on the deck having a drink in Noss Mayo. This little dinghy goes past, young chap steering and a very tasty blonde sitting at the back.

She sees us and pulls up her jumper. She had a pair of great tits I can tell you. We gave her a cheer. Then she goes all red and pulls her sweater down.

Later, as we are steering the dinghy into the quay, we saw the blonde again. This time she was sitting on a rock in a Bikini. She held up this yellow tee-shirt with a palm tree on it, same as Nobby's. She must have pulled it up with her sweatshirt when she tried to show it to us before. No wonder she blushed!

'Great!' Nobby shouts. 'But I preferred the other two!'

18

MURDER?

Poor old D. I. Baines. He really thought he'd got me last year.

An old mate of mine lives over towards Bedford; Big house, new wife, he got her from a catalogue. She doesn't speak much English but these Philipino women are real lookers. More important they know their place. Dee says they age quick. Well. I told her, you'd just send for another one in that case.

Anyway. This mate was celebrating an anniversary. If I say to you, he deals in gold, has a smelting licence and his son works at Heathrow. You might guess what he was celebrating. So I ain't telling you his name.

It was going to be a posh do so Dee hired a

long dress and made me wear a dicky bow. Looked the dog's bollocks I did, just like James Bond. The party was in a marquee on the lawn. Lot of gold and diamonds worn that night I can tell you. At about one o'clock, four of us men went into the billiard room for a game of snooker and some top-level talks.Seems our host had been robbed! He has a little place in Hatton Garden. The Wednesday before the party, two geezers dressed in black, knocked down the door with a sledgehammer. One wore a gorilla mask and the other a Mrs Thatcher. Difficult to say which one was the more scary I would think. They had a couple of sawn off shotguns, crude but effective. The gorilla and Mrs Thatcher tied the staff up and legged it with all the diamonds in the place.

Needless to say the police were not called in.

Over our game, the talk was of who had done it and who the fence was. My mate suspected his accountant had organised it. Mostly it seemed, because the bloke hadn't turned up for the party. They were making plans. About 2 o'clock I felt it was time to leave.

Serious violence isn't my thing.

Dee and I set off over the Downs for home. At the time I was driving an old Jag. Doing it up to sell on the vintage car market. It's a hobby of mine. Bloody thing died in the middle of nowhere. It had to be a fuel problem so it didn't take long for me to realise it was the petrol pump. Now, the petrol pump is in the boot on that model and you can work it by hand.

'You get in the boot.' I told Dee. 'I'll stop every so often and give you some air.'

'I am not getting' in there,' she says. 'Are you barking mad? In this ball

gown!'

'Take it off then. It's the only way we'll get home tonight.'

Worked like a dream it did.I stopped every ten minutes or so to make sure she was doing it properly. There wasn't much traffic on the road at that time of night and soon we were tucked up in bed fast asleep.

Half past five in the morning it was. Mr Baines was hammering on my front door. When I opened it, four coppers in flak jackets burst in, waving guns!

'Bloody Hell,' I thought. My mate must have done for his bookkeeper already.

Turned out that a car had passed us up on the downs, just as I opened the boot. The driver had a bit of a shock seeing Dee laid in there, dressed only in her undies. He jumped to the conclusion I was disposing of a body. The guy took the number of the Jag and reported it when he got home. Very efficient the old bill when he needs to be. Lucky for me I had done all the paper work on the Jag, tax, insurance and that. Lucky that I didn't get breathalysed the mood Baines was in.

Still. It all got sorted out in the end.

My lucky night one way and another, I heard later, the bookkeeper hadn't been so fortunate. Seems my mate and his associates wave to a certain fly-over on a certain by-pass every time they drive past.

19

GOOD IDEAS … NOT

I picked up a new motor a couple of weeks ago. I got it for Dee. She's always wanted a sports car and it was her birthday. So when I saw this M.G. advertised in the paper, sweet as a nut and a steal at the price, I snapped it up. Mal said that I could keep it up at his yard until the birthday.

We were having a heat wave at the time so I put the top down and off I went. There I was fiddling away with the radio, checking out the knobs and buttons. When I saw it in the mirror, white and red with flashing blue lights on the top. Did me for doing forty in a thirty mile an hour area.

Pig sick I was.

Since I was on the early side I called in on

Snatch to show him the car. Just as I was about to ring the bell, the front door flew open and I was knocked backwards into the hedge.

'Aaaaaaaaaargh!' Snatch charged passed me like an express train. Down the path he went and over the gate. I have never seen anyone run so fast. Could have beaten Lynford Christie. Over the road he flew and round the corner of the house opposite. I followed.

Snatch ran over the lawn. 'Aaaaaaaaagh!' Still hollering. He jumped bum first into their fishpond and disappeared from view. All was quiet, just a few bubbles on the top of the water.Then. Snatch rose, he stood up. Just like that bird on the shell coming out of the waves, but all covered in pondweed and green slime. He spat some water out.

'Bloody hell.' Snatch looked down at the water lapping round his thighs. 'Whoops.' He said.

As Snatch squelched back over the road he told me what had happened. Seems he had been mowing the lawn at the back of the house. He pushed the machine up by the side of his shed and upset some hornets minding their own business in their nest. So they had a go at him. Snatch took to his heels and the rest we know.

'Bastards!' he said as he went back into the house and plodded upstairs, water and bits falling everywhere. 'chased me they did, I'll 'ave 'em. You see.'

When he came down again. I told him how my Gramps got rid of wasp nests with a rag soaked in a bit of petrol. It smoulders and gasses them.

'I got a can of petrol.' He said. 'Come on.'

'Call of nature.' I told him, 'I'll get Mandy to give me some old rags.'

So, it was some minutes before I followed him up the garden to his shed.

Now I'm not too keen on Snatch's shed. He took to brewing his own beer some time ago. Bloody awful stuff it is. Gives you the squits as well. Though it's not as bad as his wine. The nettle is sweet and the beetroot makes you go blind after two glasses. Strange noises come from his shed; gurgling, a bit like your belly after drinking the stuff, plus all the popping and banging as the brew explodes in its bottles.

Snatch was up the side of his shed.

Between it and the next-door neighbour's

wooden fence is just enough room to get a mower up and it is right up against the back fence. The people that live behind Snatch have built a six-foot high wooden fence. So they can't see him and all his kids I should think. There was a smell of petrol. A gallon of the stuff it turns out. Snatched poured it all down the hole. Didn't bother about a rag.

Then, BOOM!Out flies Snatch, back first feet in the air. He lands on his back and looks up at me. He had the look of a Black and White Minstrel when he grinned.

'That got the bastards.'

'Yeah.' I said, 'and you haven't got no eyebrows left. No shed either by the look of it.'

The fence and the shed were ablaze.

'It sounded like a good idea to me.'

'Yes, it is, with a rag and a little petrol.' I sighed, even dumb animals learn easier than Snatch.

Snatch laughed and sat up. 'Let's get another lager.'

'Good idea.' I say. Thinking it a good idea to get away from the shed and the bottles of beer kept therein. There was a large explosion just as Ginger walked round the corner of the house.

'Jesus Snatch, you taken up bomb making?'

We sat down on some old deck chairs by the back door and watched the blaze. I made the kids stand behind us. Snatch opened a can and handed it to Ginger as more bottles began to explode in the shed. We heard the sound of fire engines in the distance. The children ran out to the front of the house. Snatch grinned.

'The kids are loving this.'

'Nice motor you got out there. '

Ginger said as we watched the flames die down.

'It's for Dee's birthday.' I waved the speeding ticket at him. 'Look at this,' I told him what had happened.

'Don't worry about that.'

Ginger took the ticket off me and ate it!

*

Well you can imagine. I had to take my documents in, didn't I? What could I do? The next day I walked up to the desk Sergeant and told him the truth. Like I said before. No sense of humour old bill. He did not find it at all amusing.

'I can't process it then.' He said. 'Court for you, old son.'

I pointed out that OK my pal had eaten my ticket but he must have the details on his computer or somewhere. Else how would he know who had to come in with their papers.

'Yes, but I'm too busy to look at the moment. So you'll have to go over there and wait.'

I sat down on one of the hard chairs and waited while he drank his tea and picked his nose. After half an hour, young Sally Bird came in asking to speak to her old man. No way would my friend the sergeant let that happen.

'And how is Tweety then?' I asked her. 'What's he been up to?'

'You ain't never going to believe it.'

Seems that Tweety and a couple of mates decided to hold up a bank. They settled on midday since people would be paying in from the market stalls, it being Friday, market day. Tweety had thought up a cunning disguise. They put brown make up on, wore black wigs, white shirts, black trousers and spoke with Indian accents. Made them look like waiters at the local Tandoori.

On the way into the bank they stuck a notice on the door saying 'closed for stocktaking' which they nicked from the front of one of the shops in the high street. Good thinking.

Tweety had done a bit more thinking. He knew one of the men working down a hole in the road outside the bank. So Tweety arranged for this geezer to cut through the electricity cable (by accident) as the three of them went into the bank. That day was the hottest day of the year. The bank didn't have any air conditioning because there was no electricity.

Tweety had shut the door and locked it.

It took Tweety and his mates sometime to get through to the staff and customers. Seems they didn't understand a word of what was said to them. Maybe because Tweety is a Scouser, he is difficult to understand at the best of times, him talking with an Indian accent must have been completely incomprehensible. The employees stood with their hands up and mouths open, fascinated. Watching the brown make up start to run down into the white shirts of the Pakistani bank robbers.

Tweety, being a bit of a closet thespian, had painted his eyebrows black. His mates liked that, so he did theirs and put black lines round all three pairs of eyes. Then he got carried away and painted on mustachios. They must have looked like something out of the silent movies. Unfortunately Tweety used his kiddies paint box.Mr Baines and D S Campbell nicked them as they were climbing over the wall at the back of the bank.

I wonder if they had an identity parade. Imagine it, a row of white men with brown make up and black paint standing in front of electric fires to make it all run.

I shall have to ask D.S. Campbell, he'd see the funny side all right.

That desk Sergeant made me wait two and a half hours.

'I suggest you choose your friends more carefully,' was his parting shot.

'Well at least I've got some friends,' I told him, 'don't suppose you have.'

I didn't hang around to hear his reply.

20

WEDDINGS

When my boy, Paul came and told me he was getting married I wasn't too surprised, Sharon being in the club.

'I 'suppose you'll be wanting me to pay for it?' I said, not minding, because I like a big knee's up. Though the invitations can be a bit tricky since I never know who's not speaking to who in my family. When they are really feuding you have to keep your head down because they tend to go after each other with shotguns. This isn't as bad as you might think since most of them are bad shots or are pissed half the time.

*

I remember we went to town on Spider's wedding. 120 people to the Church and lunch, 100 more to the supper and disco in the evening. The bride, Sue, arrived in a helicopter. Her dress was shiny white with little bits of stuff hanging off her shoulder pads. And little white skinkley things bobbing about in her hair. She had bows all round the bottom of her dress and so did the 5 bridesmaids. They were all in tangerine with bows everywhere, in their hair, on the net petticoats that stuck the dresses out and even on the backs of their orange high-heeled shoes. I expect they had bows on their knickers. And believe me it wouldn't have taken much to get a look, if you know what I mean.

Tarts, I got to say it, even if they are family.

Anyway, the Bride and Groom drove to the reception in one of my vintage cars from the field where the helicopter had to land. The pub wasn't quite ready for us when we got there, so we all had to go into the bar and wait. Cost me a fortune buying them all drinks, so when we got into the function room we were a very merry bunch.

Sue and Spider sat under an arch of

balloons and more bows. My first wife sat the other end of the table. I could smell carbolic from where I was. She had brought her own glass, spoon, knife and fork. She also had her own cushion to sit on. All the presents were on a table by the door. I knew which one was from her on the table because it smelt of Coal Tar.

Sue and Spider and the date of the wedding was printed on the napkins, place settings and matches, you name it, it was printed on it. Every guest had a white cracker (with two bows on) with a gift inside, perfume for the ladies, aftershave for the men.

Yes, it was a great day.

Three of the guests ended up in the cells for drunk and disorderly. Nobby was done for A.B.H, seems some one spilt some beer on his new

suit. And five of the young'uns were done for affray. No one can remember what they were fighting about.

Seems the party went on down the cells of the local nick.

*

Well, after that, Paul didn't want a big do. They wanted to go to Barbados. Get married on a beach, romantic like. The one good thing was his Mum, my first wife, wouldn't go.

Foreign. Dirty see?

We got a package, all inclusive, food, drink, entertainment, the wedding and the photo's. Eight of us went; Paul and Sharon, me and Dee, Sharon's Mum and Dad, The Best man and his girl friend.

Of course no one told us that August in Barbados is hot and humid, bloody hot and bloody humid. We were the third wedding that morning. We were hustled onto the beach and had to stand under what looked like a small bandstand. (The pink and cream paint needed re-doing since most of it had blistered off)

Sharon looked like a large meringue, her face being the raspberry on the top. Us men sweating in our suits. All around us were kids and people with skin ranging from pastey white to third degree burns. Two women sat on the grass dunes behind, watching us, drinking rum punches and rattling their ice cubes.

One had squeezed herself into a bikini made for a woman half her size. She was as red as a post box and covered in sun oil. The other woman was white as a sheet, dressed in shorts and a tee shirt. Her legs were covered in big red bites.No one warns you about the mosquitoes either.Then some little kid wandered up licking a chocolate ice cream. He stood between the Bride and Groom and began to talk to us all. I caught hold of his arm just as he was about to wipe his cornet across Sharon's dress. He went off howling after I told him if I saw him again I'd pull his head off. Next thing I know this big guy with sun burn on his tattoos taps me on the shoulder.

'Whadya say to my little Wayne?'

The other little boy with him says, 'it 'im Dad. Go on Dad 'it 'im.'

'Shudup Elvis.' He said and clipped Elvis round the ear.

I politely pointed out that I would be forced to give him a slap if he didn't take himself and his children away from my son's wedding. So he looked at me, the groom and the best man, clumped Elvis one for luck and shuffled back to his sun lounger. The vicar rushed through the rest of the ceremony since there were six more couples to get through. Like a sausage machine it was. Then for some reason we had to walk round the complex pushing the cake on a trolley.

*

All very different than poor old Mal's wedding, he and Tracy got married at the registry office. I was the Best Man, fucking Sharmain was the bridesmaid, Snatch and Mandy were the witnesses.

I had a big old peppermint green, Chevy at that time. So I said I'd drive the bride and groom. Mandy tied white ribbons to the car, a difficult job for her, being so fat. Nine months gone.

Early I was, which was just as well.

I parked in the yard and got out of the car. I assumed they were in the house getting ready. Then I heard banging noises coming from the Horsebox parked in the corner. As I walked towards it, Fucking Sharmain flew out. She got up, rubbed the side of her head, folded her arms and frowned. Then she stumped off saying. 'I didn't do fucking nuffin.'

'You come back 'ere.' Tracy appeared at the top of the ramp. 'Do

you 'ere me?'

'I told yer I dint fucking do it!' Sharmain shouted over her shoulder as she walked towards the house.

'She's got a fucking filthy mouth that one.'
Said Tracy jumping down to face me.

Since there was no answer to that, I said.
'You aren't getting married like that are
you?'

'I got half an hour to get ready. Where's
Mal?'

'I don't know. Where was he last?'

Perhaps he's done a runner I thought, good
man.

'He was changing the oil on my car. He's up
in the barn.'

I had to pull Mal, feet first, out from under
the engine of a battered old Horizon. He lay
on the trolley and looked up at me. Mal
looked as if he had emptied the sump all
over himself.

'I've gone blind!' he said. Which wouldn't
have been such a bad thing. Since he was
marrying Tracy.

'Take your glasses off.' The round white
patches made him look like a panda. 'Hurry
up Mal. You're getting married remember?'

'Bloody 'ell.' He says and ran for the

bungalow.Half an hour later they came out to the car. Fucking Sharmain looked like a proper little girl; pigtails, ribbons and a spotty pink dress. Tracy had a pale blue suit on with a matching hat. It was the first time I'd seen Tracy in a skirt. Come to think of it. It was the last time. Mal wore a dark blue suit that was a bit on the big side. All three of them were clean and smelling of soap.

'You got the ring?' I asked as we drove into the Registry Office car park with five minutes to spare.

'What?' They said.

'The ring! You know? The wedding ring.'

'I knew we'd forgotten something,' said Mal.

'I got one Mum.' Fucking Sharmain said as she pulled a ring off one of her fingers. 'It come out of a cracker.'

I didn't know where to look when the Registrar held out a deep red velvet cushion with gold tassels on the corners and said 'Ring?'

It looked very odd, that luminous green plastic ring with a yellow pony's head on it.

'We are gathered together...' The guy started up and so did the groaning.

It wasn't Mal. It was Mandy. Gone into labour, by the time we were out in the car park doing photos the ambulance arrived.

After the ceremony we went to the Curry House. Snatch joined us later.

'It's a boy.' He shouted as he came through the door. He tripped up the step. Said 'Whoops,' and grabbed the tablecloths of the first two tables as he went down.

The waiters took him upstairs and cleaned him up. They lent him some clothes. I bought drinks and more food for the people whose Saturday lunch had been spoiled.

We all got Delhi belly that night and Snatch named his son Mohammed.

21

RETIREMENT

I am retired from my life of crime, sort of. I buy and sell a few cars and go out in the lorry two or three days a week.

One day last month I was sitting in my cab having a sandwich and listening to the Archers. I was in a lay- by, quiet and shady on a hot day. It's surrounded by trees, which back onto the gardens of some really posh houses.

Anyway, the Archers finished and I turned the radio off. Don't care about the shipping forecast since I'm not out there, am I? I heard an alarm go off behind the trees. Didn't think anything of it. I Started up the

engine, put the wrapping back in my new
Tupperware lunch box, brushed the crumbs
off my lap, put the lorry into gear and let
the hand brake off.

Suddenly, this bloke jumps out of the
shrubbery waving a handgun at me! Little
guy he was. He took a flying leap at the cab
and hung on, shouting and swearing his
face bright red.

I switched off.'Get out.' He shouts. I
do.'Hands up.' He squeals.Up they go.The
guy is waving the gun about, practically
foaming at the mouth. He looked like a
hyperactive gnome on speed.

'You aren't going to shoot me.' I say.

'I am you bastard! I've had enough! And
enough is enough!'

'You aren't going to shoot no one with the
safety catch on.' I nod at the

gun.

'What!' He looks down at the gun with a
frown.Which gives me the chance to snatch
the gun away from him. Nice little piece it
was too.

'You gotta licence for this?' I asked as I put
the safety catch on and slipped it into my
pocket.

'No.' He collapsed in a heap whining. 'Please don't shoot. I can't stand it. Why do you keep burgling me?'

I calmed him down and the upshot was. He had been burgled five times! The getaway car always parked in this particular lay-by. So when I started up my engine, he thought it was the thieves. I pointed out that I would hardly be pulling jobs in a seventeen-ton lorry with a full load.

'Look.' I said. 'I can hear the police sirens. If I was you I wouldn't mention talking to me or the gun.' I didn't want to be dragged into it. Especially since I'm retired. (Dee would have my balls for breakfast!)

'Tell you what I'll do.' I told him. 'I've got few contacts. I'll put the word about. See if I can't put a stop to it for you.' I felt sorry for the poor bugger and I had a feeling I knew who it might be, burglarising him.

This young'un, Bazza his name is, had been trying to sell stuff in the local pubs. His Mum was an old "friend" of mine so I didn't want the lad getting his head blown off. But you never know nowadays. Spider tells me that Bazza is a 'crack head' so probably he will get topped one way or another. Crime is becoming something of a nasty business.

These kids nowadays. No Discipline, see?
They go round with knives and would pull a
gun on their Granny for a few bob.

They haven't got any sense of responsibility.

I blame the parents

I don't what the world is coming to.

I really don't.

You gotta laugh.

Printed in Great Britain
by Amazon